From Hinton
to *Hamlet*

From Hinton to *Hamlet*

BUILDING BRIDGES BETWEEN
YOUNG ADULT LITERATURE
AND THE CLASSICS

Sarah K. Herz
with Donald R. Gallo

GREENWOOD PRESS
Westport, Connecticut • London

Library of Congress Cataloging-in-Publication Data

Herz, Sarah K.
    From Hinton to *Hamlet* : building bridges between young adult
literature and the classics / Sarah K. Herz with Donald R. Gallo.
      p.   cm.
    Includes bibliographical references and index.
    ISBN 0-313-28636-1 (alk. paper)
    1. Young adult literature—Study and teaching (Secondary)
2. Literature—Study and teaching (Secondary) 3. Youth—Books and
reading. I. Gallo, Donald R. II. Title.
PN1009.A1H47 1996
809'.89283'0712—dc20   95-38657

British Library Cataloguing in Publication Data is available.

Library of Congress Catalog Card Number: 95-38657
ISBN: 0-313-28636-1

First published in 1996

Greenwood Press, 88 Post Road West, Westport, CT 06881
An imprint of Greenwood Publishing Group, Inc.

Printed in the United States of America

The paper used in this book complies with the
Permanent Paper Standard issued by the National
Information Standards Organization (Z39.48-1984).

10 9 8 7 6 5 4 3

Copyright Acknowledgments

The authors and publisher gratefully acknowledge permission for use of the following
material:

Excerpts from "Two for One: Combining Classics and Young Adult Books," by Don Gallo.
Printed with permission of the *Arizona English Bulletin*, where it appeared in Winter 1995.

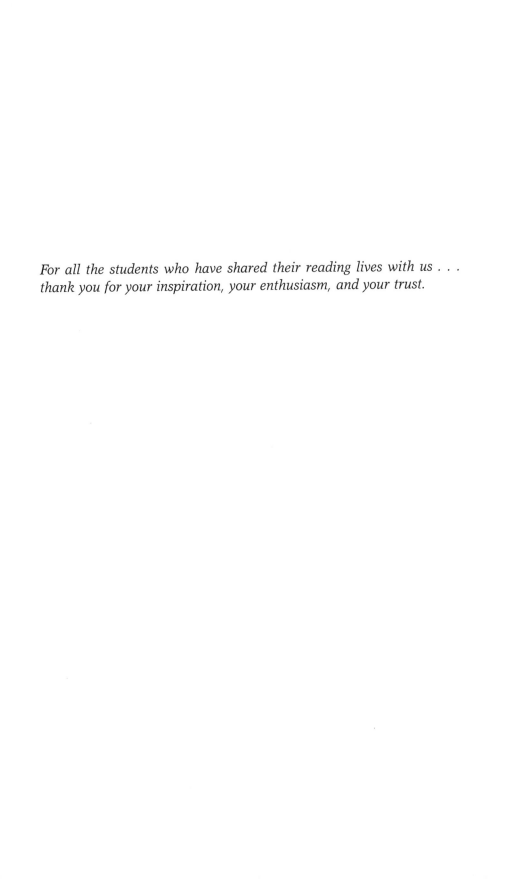

For all the students who have shared their reading lives with us . . .
thank you for your inspiration, your enthusiasm, and your trust.

CONTENTS

PREFACE

When more than one author's name is on a book, readers often want to know how much of the book was written by each one, and whether they worked side-by-side in concert or whether each person wrote different parts of the work. For the curious, let it be known that with the exception of the final two sections of Chapter 4 and all of Chapter 7, which I wrote, Sarah Herz wrote almost everything else. I handled the major editing of the book, made recommendations for rewriting, suggested additional sources, and added a bit here and there. So when you see "I" throughout this book, other than on this page, that is Sarah speaking about her experiences. Elsewhere we have used the collective "we." Thus, although this book was the result of a cooperative effort, Sarah Herz did most of the work.

Donald Gallo

ACKNOWLEDGMENTS

Thanks to the Westport School District, which in 1990 granted me a sabbatical leave that opened up the world of Young Adult Literature to me.

Thanks to the people who shared their experiences in the classroom and library with me—Barbara Blosveren, head of the Young Adult Services department of the Stratford, CT, Library Association; Marta Campbell, reference librarian, Westport, CT, Public Library; Carol Davidson, library/media specialist at O. H. Platt High School in Meriden, CT; Philip Devine, supervisor of language arts, K–12, Stratford, CT; Sandra Klimkowski, Integrated Language Arts teacher, O. H. Platt High School, Meriden, CT; Harriet Selverstone, department chair, library/media specialists, Norwalk, CT, Public Schools; and Cheryl Karp Ward, library/media specialist, Windsor Locks, CT, Middle School.

Special thanks to Margery Fisher, library/media specialist, Coleytown Middle School, Westport, CT, an extraordinary librarian who never said no to me and my English classes. She "booktalked" thousands of books for us and helped my students find pleasure and excitement in their reading lives.

Thanks to Andrew H. Smith, manager, School and Library Marketing, Bantam Doubleday Dell; Dorothy Millhofer, director of School and Library Marketing, and Gwen Montgomery, editorial director, Books for Young Readers, both at Avon Books. Your generosity in providing new books helped keep me up-to-date.

Thanks to Barbara Rader of Greenwood Press for her patience and support, and finally . . . a special thanks to Don Gallo for tolerating my erratic work habits and pushing me to complete this book.

Sarah K. Herz

July 1995

INTRODUCTION

Imagine coming into your classroom and listening to your students discussing literature—arguing about plot, discussing character development, quoting dialogue, mentioning flashback and foreshadowing! Ignoring your presence, they continue to discuss what they are reading, intense, excited, happy. Does this sound like a fantasy? It isn't.

The purpose of this book is to help teachers consider the unlimited possibilities of Young Adult Literature in the classroom. Library media specialists also will find this book useful as a source of young adult titles for teachers of language arts as well as teachers in other content areas. We want to convince you that Young Adult Literature (YAL) is a powerful tool to help students realize that reading is a pleasurable activity and to help them develop into confident, critical readers.

For too long YAL has been ignored in the English curriculum; for too long teachers have neglected to integrate YAL with the classics and other required readings. YAL's value lies in its ability to draw students' attention into the story immediately, because it deals with real problems in their own lives. It helps teenagers in their search for understanding in the complex world of today. The questions *Who am I?* and *Where do I fit in?* plague most adolescents throughout their formative years. As developing readers, many students cannot find answers to these questions in such wonderful classics as *Jane Eyre, Pride and Prejudice, Tom Jones, Green Dolphin Street, Moby Dick, Babbitt,* or *Hamlet* . . . yet.

Teachers should become aware that since 1967 the literary quality of YAL has improved dramatically. In addition to the usual literary elements of adult literature—plot, setting, point of view, characterization, dialogue, style, and theme—most YAL now includes the following characteristics:

- the main character is a teenager
- the story is often narrated by a teenager, creating an intimate contact between reader and writer
- the story is about a problem or concern with which teenage readers can identify
- the first page or two demands readers' attention, enticing them to read on
- the book is not too long (usually about 200 pages).

Teenage readers feel connected to YAL immediately for many reasons:

- they find the book interesting because they can read and understand it with ease
- they gain insights into human relationships; they begin to discover how or why human beings relate to one another
- they discuss the books with friends and discover that they understand the author's purpose.

YOUNG ADULT LITERATURE

YAL has gone through a transformation; what used to be used only as supportive reading for less able and less motivated students has become a rich literary source that meets the abilities of all types of readers. But before you begin to investigate the possibilities of YAL in your classes, if you are not already familiar with a variety of books, it is important that you confer with a school or town librarian and read several award-winning titles. Better yet, ask your students for some titles of the best books they've read in the past two years. In many instances, you will find that their favorite titles are *not* what a teacher "taught" to the whole class but rather are particular titles recommended by classmates. In checking many of my students' favorite titles with school librarians, I found that most students' choices were YAL.

Seven years ago I started reading YAL, and I haven't stopped. During those early years I learned more about the world of adolescents through these stories, poems, plays, and novels than I learned in psychology courses. And when I listened to my students discussing books, I heard the meaning they made from reading YAL. YAL liberated my classroom and me—I am no longer the authority figure dominating their reading life. But the most satisfying bonus of all is my acceptance into their discussions, seeing their willingness to risk and to trust writing and speaking their opinions in our classroom. I've learned to bridge my own reading—I read YAL along with adult books—and I too take pride in sharing my reading life with my students.

Sarah K. Herz

Chapter 1

Letting Go: How I Stopped Forcing Books down Students' Throats and Found Out What They Really Needed

Young Adult Literature entered my classroom and teaching under strange circumstances. In 1987 I was teaching half-time in middle school and half-time in senior high school. Looking back, I realize that switching back and forth between age groups was confusing and difficult for me. At best, my teaching successes were scattered that year.

However, something dynamic happened between me and my middle school students that made an enormous impact on my teaching style. Through the honesty, trust, and cooperation of my students, I discovered a treasure trove of literature that I had scoffed at and ignored for more than 15 years—Young Adult Literature. (Some refer to it as adolescent literature, or literature written for young adults.)

LITERARY SNOBBERY

Like many secondary teachers of English, I had not read Young Adult Literature (YAL) in years. In fact, I was a literary snob—anything I taught had to be a classic that would enable students to understand the purpose of great literature. Great literature meant the classics, the classics as prescribed in the curriculum guide, a guide that was compiled over 25 years earlier with few new titles. And every student had to read these classics to become an educated person. (I know I was not alone in my attitude.)

My initial contact with YAL had led me to believe that most of the novels were escapist, sentimental confessions with little or no literary merit. I remembered my students in seventh, eighth, and ninth grade raving about S. E. Hinton's ~~The Outsiders, Rumblefish, and That Was Then,~~ *This Is Now*. I had skimmed *The Outsiders* and was appalled that my students, many of them honor roll members, could call this good literature. I read *Rumblefish* and my opinion did not change. And some YAL titles were ridiculous—*Rumblefish! Mom, the Wolfman and Me! Dinky Hocker Shoots Smack!* Why were suburban kids interested in stories about gangs, divorce, and drugs?

And the covers were garish! They reminded me of the covers of sleazy detective novels. Their most positive quality was their ability to grab the attention of nonreaders, because they dealt with subject matter that was of interest to that particular group. There was no place in our curriculum for these kinds of books, I maintained. They did not "fit in" with such classics as Shakespeare's *A Midsummer Night's Dream* or *The Odyssey, Of Mice and Men, Men of Iron, Hiroshima,* or *Great Expectations.*

But thanks to a determined group of seventh and eighth graders in 1987, my 1970s attitude about YAL changed. Their serious purpose and cooperation taught me to read, to discuss, and to respect the literary qualities of novels and stories written for young adults.

STUDENT REBELLIONS

My moment of epiphany with Young Adult Literature came when we were trying to get through *Lilies of the Field*. My seventh graders were hostile and quite literally refused to discuss or read the book. We met after my morning at the senior high and after their lunch, so the classroom atmosphere was charged; there was lots of anger floating around the room, most of it directed at me. *What right did I have to force this lousy book down their throats?* they demanded. *What about their rights?* I thought they were a bunch of crabby kids, unwilling to cooperate.

Somehow we slogged through *Lilies*. They made a "deal" with me—they would finish *Lilies* if they could pick out their next reading book and be allowed to read in class two periods a week. I added two requirements— (1) they had to discuss the book with the class; in other words, one or two or three students could read the same book, and they could present the book to the class (we called this Book Forum), and (2) they had to write a response to the book in their reading journal. We reached agreement— too easily, I thought to myself. Because they had not shown any enthusiasm about reading and discussing literature during the short story unit or *Lilies* after nine weeks of school, I wasn't too optimistic about our agreement.

Since I did not have a classroom library, we went to the school library after I had conferred with the librarian, Margery Fisher, who was very cooperative. She loaned me professional library journals so I could read monthly book reviews of recommended literature for adolescents, which also featured interesting articles by teachers and librarians about books teenagers were reading. Although I was a long-time subscriber to the *English Journal*, published by the National Council of Teachers of English, I paid little or no attention to the monthly column "Books for the Teenage Reader." (Now it's the first article I turn to.) The librarian also gave me annotated lists of recently published books that were in the school library. From our lengthy conversation I knew I had found a knowledgeable resource who was au courant about YAL. And because she had been the librarian for 20 years, she knew which titles were on the shelves. She also knew which titles circulated among students—which books were "hot." (Word-of-mouth is the best recommendation among students.)

I scheduled a period for both classes and she agreed to pull books—mysteries, fantasy, survival, Gothic—by YAL authors as well as well-known adult authors such as Agatha Christie, Jack London, John Hersey, and Mark Twain. During our scheduled period she booktalked a lot of current YAL, briefly describing the plot and characters from various stories to pique students' interests. Some of the titles were: *The Goats* by Brock Cole, *Where It Stops, Nobody Knows* by Amy Ehrlich, *Dicey's Song* by Cynthia Voigt, *Hatchet* by Gary Paulsen, *The Year without Michael* by Susan Beth Pfeffer, *Park's Quest* by Katherine Paterson, and *Fallen Angels* by Walter Dean Myers. She did a terrific job. Our session generated a lot of enthusiasm among the students. In fact, shopping at the library seemed almost as interesting as shopping at the mall. Some students checked out soft covers, some hard covers; some even checked out several books.

A CHANGE IN ATMOSPHERE

The atmosphere in my classroom changed. Most important, the students decided what *they* wanted to read, and *their* attitude about reading changed because they read during class. Reading became an in-class activity as well as an outside activity. On days when we read in class (I read and wrote with students at all times), I can't remember any discipline problems—it was quiet, reading was going on! As I sat looking around the classroom, I kept thinking to myself that I was really dense—why had it taken me 15 years to let go? What was happening in my classroom at that moment was the best I could hope to achieve in any class!

Most of the students' reading selections were stories about adolescents dealing with real-life problems, such as friends/peers, family, school, or death. The literature offered them fictional or nonfictional experiences from which they could gain insights about their own relationships with people and the world, and from which they could test their own beliefs and values. They read science fiction, mysteries, fantasies, and historical novels, too. Some of their favorite titles were *Go Ask Alice* (by an anonymous author),

The Cage by Ruth Sendar, *Hatchet* by Gary Paulsen, *Interstellar Pig* by William Sleator, *One-Eyed Cat* by Paula Fox, *Lord of the Rings* by J.R.R. Tolkien, *Tom Sawyer* by Mark Twain, *Summer of My German Soldier* by Bette Greene, *Call of the Wild* by Jack London, *Eric* by Doris Lund, *Killing Mr. Griffin* by Lois Duncan, and *The Hitchhiker's Guide to the Galaxy* by Douglas Adams.

Their interest, their excitement, their reactions to the books showed me that they were capable, confident, independent readers who took pride in choosing their own literature. Their written and oral responses convinced me more and more that this literature was crucial to their reading development. Some of their comments revealed wonderful insights about their reading:

I could hear the main character's voice in my head. I feel as if I was with him as he ran away with his best friend. (*The Outsiders* by S. E. Hinton)

I exploded after I was done with this novel . . . it was so full of suspicion in the beginning and when the end came it was very startling. (*Interstellar Pig* by William Sleator)

This story tells the plain truth about the ups and downs of living a life on drugs. I constantly find myself saying to her as I read the diary "what's wrong with you, how could you go back? Don't you know you are killing yourself?" The point of this book is to tell people that life is too precious to waste. The most important phrase in this book is "anyone that says drugs are not addictive, they're lying to you." (*Go Ask Alice*)

I had a chance to observe some patterns in reading that were most interesting. Students recommended books to each other; there was great pride in "selling" a title. Book Forum was an exciting, informative method for them to convince peers to read the titles they had read. Their comments were insightful and critical; they spontaneously used such literary references as character and plot development, foreshadowing, dialogue, flashback, description, and narration. They recalled other titles with similar plot sequences and characters and compared the titles. And they grasped and explored all these ideas without teacher-led questions!

The students also developed mutual respect for the limitations of various readers. And their literature discussion eliminated social barriers; that is, they exchanged ideas without thinking about student social groups. Everyone was a lot kinder to and more respectful of each other; they listened, questioned, and applauded during Book Forum. Their written responses, based on a choice of questions I handed out, were honest, critical, thoughtful. Although students read adult titles too, the majority of titles read were Young Adult Literature. As I reflect on the exciting and stimulating atmosphere in those classrooms, I am certain that the catalyst was the quality of Young Adult Literature my students eagerly read and wrote about with ease and confidence.

VALUING STUDENTS' JUDGMENTS

I began to wonder whether YAL was the pathway for my students to discover and appreciate the required classic titles in our curriculum. Their joy and pleasure in reading and discussing books had changed the environment of our classroom; it was relaxed, reasonable, respectful—all the good qualities teachers try to engender. As I left the high school each day, I knew that those seventh and eighth grade classes were the highlights of my afternoon. Were these the same kids who had given me a hard time after lunch? What an amazing change! By allowing them to choose their own reading books, I had gained peace of mind along with a group of enthusiastic readers and responsive students. And they introduced me to some wonderful authors—Sue Ellen Bridgers, Virginia Hamilton, Paula Fox, Walter Dean Myers, Gary Paulsen, and the list could go on and on. I understood why they loved reading these YAL authors—their words touch the hearts and minds of adolescents.

Reading became valued and important in our classroom. And talking and writing about what students read was no longer private; they liked to share and they took pride in their opinions. Every student in those classes was responsible and honest about the books he or she read. However, I was free, too. I was not trying to be in control of their selections; I was not judgmental about what they read. By respecting their choices in reading and allowing them to discuss and write their reactions to different kinds of books, plays, short stories, poetry, biography, or nonfiction, I learned that students at various reading levels know what they want to read and what they don't want to read and have valid opinions.

I also learned that my students will find pleasure in reading, will value reading, if I listen to their reactions to what they read. And when I read what they read, I learned to appreciate the honesty and wonder of their responses. Best of all, I was no longer an authority figure in the classroom. And even today, when a student runs up to me in the hall or classroom and says, "Mrs. Herz, you've got to read this book," I feel proud to be included in her or his reading life. I feel proud inwardly, too, because I know these students value and enjoy reading literature, and they are developing as critical readers. "Letting go" can be an empowering experience for teachers and students.

It took me several years to realize that in some ways I denied my students their right to experience reading as a pleasurable activity. I was convinced that my job as a classroom teacher was to make sure they read the "right stuff." And I believed I was the person to determine what the "right stuff" was. As a beginning teacher I used to tell my ninth graders that when they were adults whizzing through O'Hare Airport on business trips, I wanted to make sure they would buy the "right titles" to read. (I read somewhere that O'Hare Airport sells the largest number of soft-cover books.) What an arrogant attitude! Some of those students are now in their thirties, and I wish I could tell them that I am thankful if they are readers at all. Whose reading life is it, anyway?

What I have come to realize is that my goals as a teacher of English are to convince students that reading can be a pleasurable activity and that they can become confident readers, capable of understanding a wide variety of literature. Using YAL in my classes these past few years has helped change the negative attitudes of nonreaders as well as average and high ability readers. Using Young Adult Literature was the starting point, the key to changing students' reading habits.

We encourage our students to open their minds to new ideas or to new types of literature while oftentimes we maintain the status quo. My own experiences with some secondary teachers at conferences and workshops lead me to believe that unless a teacher values the opportunity to encourage students to become readers, YAL doesn't have a chance in his or her classroom. And there are some teachers who will not consider YAL for fear of watering down the curriculum or diluting the importance of the classics.

As a teacher and lover of literature, I too prize the classics; but I also prize helping my students to find pleasure in reading, helping them to become critical readers, and helping them to become lifetime readers. However, if we force our students to read *The Scarlet Letter*—and quiz and test them to make sure they are reading it, and then assign a structured analytical essay, complete with thesis topics—and our students find no pleasure in reading or discussing that novel (maybe even hating it), what have we accomplished? Will they ever want to reread it later in life when they are more mature readers? Will they be inspired to read any of Hawthorne's other works? Will they recommend the story of Hester Prynne to their friends and younger siblings? Will they relate some of the themes of *The Scarlet Letter* to contemporary society? Will they ever consider it an important reading event? Or will they remember it as an agony in their literary reading life? Indeed, if we give them a steady diet of literature they do not find enjoyable and do not become emotionally involved in, will they want to read *anything* associated with an English class?

By offering students a wide variety of Young Adult Literature—and there is a wide variety in both subject matter and sophistication in today's YAL—and allowing them to choose what they want to read, you will begin to see changes in your students' attitudes about reading. For many nonreaders, whether of high, average, or low ability, YAL can be a first step in discovering a lifetime of reading.

Chapter 2

WHAT IS YOUNG ADULT LITERATURE ANYWAY? CAN IT BE ANY GOOD IF STUDENTS LIKE IT?

WHAT YOUNG ADULT LITERATURE IS AND IS NOT

Trying to explain or define Young Adult Literature to teachers who have not read it or who have a negative attitude about it (like I did initially) is very difficult. It's even more difficult because in today's supermarkets and in many bookstores what you see dominating the shelves in the Young Adult section are teen romances, Sweet Valley High stories, mysteries, and horror series written by R. L. Stine, Christopher Pike, Diane Hoh, and several others. Yes, these are Young Adult novels. But there are lots of better books that sell less well—books that would sell better if English and reading teachers knew about them and used them in their classrooms.

YAL has gone through a transformation during the past 25 years. It's important to review the changes in YAL in order to become familiar with the literary quality of current Young Adult books and to appreciate the style of writing they present.

In a 1992 article from the *Journal of Youth Services in Libraries* entitled "The Literary Value of the Young Adult Novel," Robert C. Small, Jr., summarizes the history of Young Adult novels in the twentieth century. Small, who is dean of the College of Education and Human Development at Radford University and coeditor of *The ALAN Review*, points out that many books attracted teenagers by default during the 1920s–1950s. Adults, he reminds us, "rarely chose to read the car, sports, and romance novels of that period or the many novels that appeared as part of a series, such as those featuring the adventures of Frank Merriwell, the Rover Boys, Tom Swift, the Hardy Boys, or Nancy Drew" (278). Those novels were "squeaky clean"—that is, they avoided controversial topics such as sexuality, substance abuse, and death. They focused on one socioeconomic class, for the most part—white middle-class teenagers engaged in white middle-class activities. They were considered superficial by many literary critics because they lacked credibility in portraying the true nature of adolescents' lives.

In *Literature for Today's Young Adults* (1989), which provides a comprehensive overview of YAL, Ken Donelson and Alleen Nilsen mention some authors from this earlier period whose books "stand out for their psychological perception and exceptional writing talent" (541). Among them are Maureen Daly, author of *Seventeenth Summer* (1942); John Tunis, author of sports novels such as *Iron Duke* (1938); and Henry Gregor Felsen, who in the early 1950s wrote about teenage pregnancy in *Two and the Town* and teenage accident victims in *Hot Rod* (1950), *Street Rod* (1953), and *Crash Club* (1958). These authors are important historically, because their books were written specifically for Young Adult readers. Esther Forbes's *Johnny Tremain* (1943) was written specifically for teenagers too; this Newbery Award–winning historical novel is still read in classrooms today.

But the turning point in YAL came in the late 1960s and early 1970s with the publication of S. E. Hinton's *The Outsiders* (1967), which describes the problems of alienated youth; *The Contender* (1967) by Robert Lipsyte, which reflects the hope and the despair of African-American urban youths; and *The Chosen* (1967) by Chaim Potok, which describes the inner conflicts of two Jewish adolescents. These are but a few of the many novels that changed the focus of YAL because the authors addressed the realities of teenage life and offered readers an honest view of the main characters' hopes, fears, and dilemmas.

It is important to note that as YAL gained popularity among teenage readers, the literary talents of the authors also became more evident. YAL authors incorporated into their books the same elements as those in adult novels: a consistent point of view, a significant setting, a well-delineated although relatively simple plot, vivid characterization, realistic and lively dialogue, and an attractive style.

Small points out some characteristics that are unique to Young Adult novels. Important ones are:

- the main character is a teenager
- events and problems in the plot are related to teenagers
- the main character is the center of the plot
- dialogue reflects teenage speech, including slang
- the point of view presents an adolescent's interpretation of events and people
- the teenage main character is usually perceptive, sensitive, intelligent, mature, and independent

- the novel is short, rarely more than 200 pages
- the actions and decisions of the main characters are major factors in the outcome of the conflict (282–283).

Using Small's extensive list of Young Adult (YA) novel characteristics, and comparing them with the elements of adult fiction, we begin to realize that many YAL authors, such as Robert Cormier, Walter Dean Meyers, Ouida Sebestyen, Alden R. Carter, Sue Ellen Bridgers, Chris Crutcher, and Cynthia Rylant, reflect mastery of the novel form combined with well-crafted writing. As Small points out, "Critical standards for judging the quality of young adult novels may be created by applying each of the [preceding] characteristics to one or more of the elements used in judging the novel form in general" (283).

Donelson and Nilsen define Young Adult Literature as "anything that readers between the approximate ages of twelve and twenty choose to read (as opposed to what they may be coerced to read for class assignments)" (13). Others define it as books whose main characters are teenagers, or books written specifically for a teenage audience.

Some people include in YAL the books written for adults that are read by both adults and young adults. An example of this type of "crossover" novel is J. D. Salinger's *The Catcher in the Rye* (1951). Did Salinger write this book primarily for young adults? Which age group mostly reads this book? Another example is Bobbie Ann Mason's *In Country*, which was nominated for the National Book Award in 1988. Salinger and Mason do not write for young adult readers per se; publishers categorize these novels as adult novels. But they appeal to young adult readers because they include some of the YA novel characteristics mentioned previously.

Regardless of the conflicting points of view among teachers, librarians, critics, and publishers, there is clearly a distinct body of literature written specifically for young adults and being read by them.

TRADITIONAL USES OF YOUNG ADULT LITERATURE

These books can be used by teachers in a variety of ways. The most widely accepted model involves using YAL as supportive reading or as an alternative literature curriculum for lower-level English classes. Another model involves the use of YAL by the supportive reading teacher, who will have a library of YAL and other softcover books to meet the needs of those students who cannot or will not read the "classic texts" taught by the English teacher. These novels are considered less demanding and more appropriate for the needs of those students.

These models reinforce the notion that YAL is for the remedial reader, or the nonmotivated reader who cannot handle the prescribed readings in the English curriculum. Based on some teachers' classroom experiences, these novels are ideal for low ability readers, students with short attention spans who cannot engage in traditional classroom literature. Although the teacher accepts the YA books or other titles as an alternative, it's fair to assume that the teacher is accommodating the needs of the students and does not consider the titles comparable to the "normal" class texts. Thus YAL, like some stock character actor, is typecast by many teachers as being inferior reading and lacking the necessary qualities of great works of literature. Many teachers equate YAL with boxed sets of controlled vocabulary reading books, sometimes referred to as "hi-lo" books, with no literary qualities.

This attitude about YAL is further reinforced because the traditional secondary school English curriculum in most schools has not included many—if any—YAL titles. A fairly recent and extensive study of the top ten titles taught in public, private, and parochial schools, grades 9–12, by Arthur N. Applebee at the Center for the Learning and Teaching of Literature at the State University of New York, Albany, confirms that traditional classics dominate the English curriculum. Comparing his 1989 survey with a 1963 survey, Applebee concludes that "Shakespeare dominated the list in 1963 and continues to do so." The only title to have dropped in popularity is *Silas Marner*! Titles that remain in the top ten are: Shakespeare's *Macbeth, Julius Caesar, Hamlet, Romeo and Juliet; The Adventures of Huckleberry Finn* by Twain; *The Scarlet Letter* by Hawthorne; *Of Mice and Men* by Steinbeck; *The Great Gatsby* by Fitzgerald; *Lord of the Flies* by Golding; and *To Kill a Mockingbird* by Lee.

These findings corroborate the case in many senior high schools. Until recently, the only new YA novels that colleagues in my school adopted for the ninth grade during the past 20 years were Robert Cormier's *The Chocolate War* and Glendon Swarthout's *Bless the Beasts and Children*. Although I frequently heard teachers state a need for more appropriate literature for average ninth and tenth grade classes, the traditional classics remained in use. Although I heard a distraught colleague swear she would never again teach Dickens's *Great Expectations* to an average-level tenth grade class, I found that most of us ignored YAL, didn't even attempt to consider it viable in the English curriculum, and if it was mentioned, assumed it was appropriate for seventh and eighth graders—definitely *not* for high school and *not* for the college-bound. Among many secondary teachers this attitude still exists today.

Over the past 20 years many authors of YAL have proven their literary worth by telling their stories from an adolescent's point of view and drawing readers immediately into the story, whether the story is fantasy, mystery, science fiction, romance, or survival. An example of the kind of writing that grabs adolescents follows, from *Chinese Handcuffs* by Chris Crutcher:

Dear Preston,
Gotta tell you this feels weird. I got the idea from a book called *The Color Purple*,
by a lady named Alice Walker. It's a good book—a really good book—but that's
not the point. The main character didn't have anyone in the world to talk to, no
one she could trust, so she started writing letters to God, because It (that's the
pronoun she used for God because she wasn't all that sure of His or Her gender)
was about the only thing left she believed in. Since you've been gone, I've been
running around so full of that day and everything that probably led up to it that
if I don't tell somebody about it, I might just explode. Only there's no one to tell.
I can't burden Dad with it; he certainly has enough other things to worry about,
what with Mom and Christy having left.(4)

Crutcher's use of an adolescent first-person narrator writing a letter to his
dead brother about his life, their father, their mother and sister, mentioning he's ready to explode, is powerful. The narrator, Dillon, draws the
reader in by sharing his most intimate feelings about death, love, fear, and
insecurities. Crutcher sustains this intimate style with his readers, reas-
suring them that their "roller coaster" feelings are not unique among their
age group. The novel is well written, characters are well developed, and
through Dillon's struggle Crutcher succeeds in proving that adolescents
can survive if they learn to compromise in an immoral world.

THEMES AND ARCHETYPES IN NOVELS
FOR YOUNG ADULTS

YAL deals with many universal themes, including the eternal questions
Who am I? and *Where do I fit in?* Some of the themes are: alienation from
one's society or group; survival or meeting a challenge; social and/or
political concerns about racial or ethnic discrimination; social concerns
about AIDS, teenage pregnancy, divorce, substance abuse, family conflicts, dealing with death, and political injustice. These are issues and
topics that *all* students can benefit from reading and discussing, not just
students at lower academic levels.

Like classics or current adult fiction, some YAL includes a variety of
situational archetypes such as the test/trial as a rite of passage, the journey
or quest of the hero, birth/death/rebirth, and the search for self. Character
archetypes such as the wise old man or woman, the sacrificial redeemer,
the hero, the matriarch/patriarch, and the innocent child are recognizable
in many stories.

Like adult best sellers, some of the literature is intended for pure escape
or entertainment, while other stories are grounded in more universal
themes. Like adult fiction and nonfiction, the structure and style of the
writing can be simple or complex. And according to current research, as
the next chapter will show, YAL has proven to be an effective means to
motivate adolescents to read all kinds of literature, including the classics.

WHY TEACH YOUNG ADULT LITERATURE?

YAL is not a stepchild of the classics or of contemporary literature. Furthermore, if our students want to read and discuss and write about YAL, don't their opinions warrant consideration? If some of our goals are to help students become lifetime readers and to help them realize the importance of literature in understanding themselves in relation to the complexities of their world, don't we need to use all the resources available to us? To engage today's students in reading, we need to consider quality adolescent literature as a means to meet the needs of those individuals in our English classes who are not reading—especially students of average or high ability who choose not to read, and students who have not developed any interest in reading literature since they were in middle school. (In the next chapter we will explore some relevant research about the reading habits of adolescents.) We are not advocating that Young Adult Literature replace the classics entirely; rather, we are asking you to consider the possibility of using some YAL, at least as an entry or bridge to the prescribed plays, novels, short stories, and essays in your curriculum.

Chapter 3

Directing versus Exploring:
How to Get to Where You're Going
without a Literary Map

TEACHING WHAT A BOOK "MEANS"

In the traditional English class, most teachers want students to acquire knowledge about literary genres, such as novels, short stories, drama, essays, poetry. We want students to be able to identify the elements of literature: setting, character, plot, style, theme. We want them to become familiar with literary terms such as *crisis, climax, foreshadowing, flashback, figurative language, denouement*. When the whole class reads a title from the traditional curriculum, we pointedly ask questions related to this literary knowledge, often in preparation for a test. Some teachers produce chapter-by-chapter study questions, which students must answer on a daily basis. In a sense these questions are telling students what is important, how they should comprehend the novel, and what the book "means."

Although the teacher believes he or she is being helpful in giving students these materials, in fact by discussing the answers to these questions on a daily basis the teacher has stolen the students' freedom to express their personal reactions to the novel. Students have not revealed their own discoveries about the novel through their private reading, nor have they been allowed to share their ideas or personal reactions with other students. In this type of English class, the teacher has transmitted what he or she (or the accompanying curriculum guide) considers the "correct interpretation" of the novel; the teacher's interpretation might be based on literary criticism, college coursework, or publishers' teaching guides. If the students do well on the teacher's test, then the teacher concludes that those students have acquired literary knowledge. The teacher probably feels good about this type of teaching experience, thinking he or she has fulfilled the goal of teaching students to understand and appreciate a work of literature.

Granted, this example might sound extreme, but teaching guides and teacher-led interpretations of prescribed curriculum titles are more the rule than the exception in our profession. The template of "teach and test" exists in too many English classes. Some teachers know what they want students to learn from a work of literature before the first paragraph, stanza, or act has been read. There are expected answers to teacher-generated questions. And the goal most of us have in mind is to assist, help, force, and convince our students to appreciate *good* literature, whatever *good* means. Early on our students get a clear message from us: if they want to be considered literate and educated adults, they must learn to appreciate *good* literature. Enjoyment of reading is not a consideration; discovery and exploration by students are immaterial; and allowing them to select what they want to read or are interested in is ignored by many of us. Our own love of reading and literature presupposes that what we select and what we interpret is best for our students. Too often reading for pleasure is not a goal, and students' opinions are immaterial.

Many of us are convinced that we are leading our students into appreciation of traditional literature, but there is qualitative and quantative research to prove us wrong. Two reader surveys reflect the effects of traditional literature on students' reading attitudes as well as their reactions to prescribed traditional assignments.

WHAT STUDENTS SAY ABOUT REQUIRED BOOKS

G. Robert Carlsen and Anne Sherrill's book *Voices of Readers: How We Come To Love Books* (1988) reveals a wide array of responses from individuals about their reading experiences in junior and senior high school. One adult reports:

During my high school days, I read most of the classroom assignments, but was bored by the masterpieces, or perhaps I failed to understand them. They seemed to be written in another language and seemed not to entertain, but confuse. (132)

Another individual recalls:

I hated almost all of the books we studied in English classes . . . I hated Charlotte Brontë the most. I was to read *Jane Eyre* for a seventh grade book report, but I couldn't finish it and have never been able to force myself to try it again. (131)

Carlsen and Sherrill's respondents cited numerous reasons for not enjoying assigned literature, including the difficulty of understanding the reading in the first place, then having to dissect the texts, "rehashing the same material for days," and having to search for the "meaning" the teacher expected, without acknowledging their own feelings, and being forced to read sophisticated texts when the students lacked the experience and maturity to fully understand them (129–136).

Donald R. Gallo, professor of English at Central Connecticut State University, studied the reading interests of nearly 3,400 students in grades four through twelve in over 50 schools in 37 towns throughout Connecticut in 1982. In his study, students were asked if they liked the novels and other books they were assigned to read. Gallo reports:

In junior high schools, 40 percent of the boys and 35 percent of the girls indicated that they *seldom* or *never* liked required selections. In senior high schools, 41 percent of the boys and 23 percent of the girls said *seldom* or *never*. In comparison, only one student in every five *usually* or *always* liked the assigned books. ("Listening to Readers," 20)

Many of the students surveyed by Gallo noted the same reaction to the classics as did the respondents in the Carlsen/Sherrill study. The Connecticut students complained that the traditional classics were "antiquated," contained unfamiliar words, and were too historical, old-fashioned, and dull. One tenth grade boy exclaimed, "These books have nothing to do with me," and a tenth grade girl commented, "Reading literature is keeping in touch with the dead." Many students agreed with another tenth grader who stated, "Our teacher doesn't *want* you to enjoy literature; she wants you to read it for the details and themes" (20). As a teacher who loves literature, I cringe at these comments and wonder how many of my students feel the same way.

Shouldn't a major purpose in teaching literature be to help students find pleasure in reading and to become lifetime readers? Certainly the above comments are convincing reasons to modify the traditional literature curriculum in order to meet the needs of students who are not yet ready for the classics.

We can best help nonreading, turned-off, bored students by first trying to understand where they are developmentally. To do so, it will help to review G. Robert Carlsen's research about the stages of developing readers, Louise Rosenblatt's transactional theory about the reader and the literary text, and Robert Probst's observations about the student's personal response to literature as a first step in understanding students' ability to make meaning or take meaning from literature.

STAGES OF GROWTH IN LITERARY APPRECIATION

G. Robert Carlsen's *Books and the Teenage Reader* (1980) explains the idiosyncratic reading patterns of adolescent readers based on their emotional and intellectual development. Carlsen, a former professor of English at the University of Iowa, based his conclusions on his own experiences with students in Iowa public schools. His theories are significant because they consider the psychological and/or social development of adolescents and their impact on students' reading choices. Carlsen matched story choices with particular age groups in order to begin to make sense of adolescents' preferences. For example, in early adolescence, between the ages of 11 and 14 years, Carlsen found the most favored types of stories were about animals, adventure, mystery, the supernatural, sports, home and family life, broad slapstick, fantasy, and historical settings. At age 15 or 16 the reading interests among Carlsen's students included nonfiction accounts of adventure, historical novels, mystical romances, and stories of adolescent life. By late adolescence, during the last two years of high school, students chose books read by adults as well as books written for teenagers. Some of the subject matter included the search for personal values, topics of social significance, strange human experiences, and the transition to adult life (36–42).

Carlsen's description of stages of reading development makes sense to us based on our own classroom experiences with student readers. In a 1974 *English Journal* article titled "Literature Is," Carlsen cites reading patterns that have been mapped through observations of thousands of adolescent subjects. He proposes five stages of developing readers:

1. *unconscious delight:* the typical response of elementary to middle school readers. They read for enjoyment without analyzing why; they have not yet developed a vocabulary for discussing emotional responses.

2. *living vicariously:* action and escape seem to dominate for middle school and junior high readers—horror, mystery, romance, fantasy, and true adventures.

3. *seeing oneself:* the typical response of readers in junior high school into high school is more egocentric. Now readers are concerned with what's happening in their personal and social lives. Young Adult Literature has a strong appeal at this stage.

4. *philosophical speculations:* upper-level high school students shift from focusing on self to an interest in others; looking for relationships; examining why. Some are still reading stories of adolescent life.

5. *aesthetic delight:* in late high school to adulthood, readers have acquired critical awareness and begin to recognize universal themes. By this stage readers have developed the vocabulary to describe literary elements. They can delight in, recognize, and appreciate the qualities of writing. (23–27)

These stages describe the norm. Students with reading problems and lower social and intellectual abilities may reach these levels at a later age. Conversely, students with stronger reading and social abilities may attain high levels sooner.

In one way, these stages build on one another; in another way, all five levels of response can operate at the same time in varying degrees. As readers, we float among the various stages of development, depending on the subject matter. It is doubtful that as educated adults we respond on an aesthetic level consistently; after all, we all like to relax with a good escapist story we don't have to ponder, just for the fun of it. We often lose ourselves in best sellers by such well-known authors as Michael Crichton, Stephen King, Robert Ludlum, John LeCarré, Susan Isaacs, or Judith Krantz. Yet many of us expect our students to respond continually at an aesthetic level to adult-oriented literature even though some of them have not matured beyond the "personal problem" stage, or lack the advanced reading skills necessary to handle many of the classics included in the traditional curriculum (e.g., *The Scarlet Letter*, *Hamlet*, *Great Expectations*, *Ethan Frome*, *The Great Gatsby*, or *The Grapes of Wrath*). Thus, when we select literature for our classes we need to consider our students' stages of reading development. And we need to remember that students move among these various reading stages, depending on the subject matter, the genre, and their interest level as well as their individual reading ability and habits.

Accepting Carlsen's stages of literary development does not mean that we have to provide an entire curriculum suited to students' tastes (goodness, that could mean reading six consecutive R. L. Stine or Stephen King novels!); but it does mean that we ought to provide a *comfort* level in students' reading choices by providing *quality* literature that is *accessible* to them regardless of whether it fulfills *our* notion of what great literature is.

Whether *we* feel more comfortable teaching the classics is not a prime consideration if we truly want our students to enjoy reading and to become habitual readers. Too often in the past, we have graduated students from our high schools who have read the required classics and passed the obligatory quizzes and tests but who never read a significant literary work—or even a contemporary best seller—during the remainder of their lives. We have taught them the best literature of the past, but we have failed to help them become lovers of literature. By what we require them to read and how we teach it, we have failed to convince them of the power of literature to help them learn about themselves or to help them survive in a complex world.

But how will they learn to interpret and appreciate literature if they don't study the best that literature has to offer? The first step involves helping them to become readers, to enjoy the act of reading, and to realize that reading is experiential. Through their reading experiences they can begin to understand the nature of human relationships; they can begin to conjecture and to explore some answers about their primary question— *Who am I?*

Young Adult Literature provides teenagers an opportunity to read books that speak to them; these books allow the reader to compare himself or herself to the struggles of the main character. Sometimes the story exemplifies the very problem that the reader has been wrestling with and is unable to see objectively. By allowing students to read a wide variety of Young Adult Literature, as well as adult contemporary and classic literature, we are saying, "Pick what you like to read, what you are comfortable with, and enjoy a good read." And by supporting their choices, we are helping them move through their own personal maturation as serious, committed readers. This process encourages independence and respect for the individual reader and helps them to understand how literature might be useful in their struggle to comprehend the complexities in human relationships and contemporary society.

TRANSACTIONAL THEORY

It will further our understanding of students' engagement in the reading of literature if we consider two seminal works by Louise Rosenblatt, professor emeritus of English Education at New York University. Her first text, *Literature as Exploration* (first published in 1938), emphasizes the importance of the literary experience in the education of the student. Among the important theories she advances is the notion that literature teaches the student about his or her culture, that stories of America and its people offer the student a variety of opportunities to learn about America and its diverse population. The literary experience also helps the student to develop sensitivity and understanding about the human condition; it relates experiences that aid the emotional maturation of the developing reader and allows him or her to listen to and exchange ideas with other students. However, Rosenblatt adds: "Like the beginning reader, the adolescent needs to encounter literature for which he possesses the intellectual, emotional, and experiential equipment" (1983, 26). When the student uses past experiences to respond to literature, he or she is in the process of building new experiences as a guide to understanding society. Rosenblatt emphasizes the need to encourage the student to feel free to respond on an emotional as well as a judgmental level. As the students exchange their responses with other students, they begin to clarify, to reconsider, or to reaffirm their personal responses. In this atmosphere the students are making personal meaning from reading literature and are beginning to participate in the exploration of the powerful ideas transmitted by literature. But Rosenblatt warns: "Books must be provided that hold out some link with the young reader's past and present occupations, anxieties, ambitions" (72). And it is in this context that we must consider accommodating the needs of developing adolescent readers.

In her book *The Reader, the Text, the Poem* (1978), Rosenblatt explains the process of reading as a *transaction* between the reader and the text; she believes that a work of literature has no meaning to the reader until he or she has experienced a personal response. It is important to consider this explanation carefully, because many students in traditional classrooms are not offered the opportunity to have a personal response. Instead, they are lectured to or they study and accept selected literary criticism; in many cases they become passive receptors of teachers' lectures. If we consider Rosenblatt's thought-provoking explanation about the act of reading, it becomes clear to us that we must allow our students to become active readers.

Using "poem" to refer to the "whole category of aesthetic transactions between readers and text," Rosenblatt describes the poem "as an event in time . . . during a coming-together, a compenetration, of a reader and a text" (1978, 12). The words of the literature enter a student's consciousness and tap into his or her personal experience. The words and the reader's experiences begin a process of meaning that evokes a personal response in the reader. This meaning is highly personal, asserts Rosenblatt; until it is shared, it remains a private meaning. It is not likely to coincide with teacher meaning or critic meaning or any other imposed meaning. But its importance is the first step in the reader's "reading life"; it must be accepted and respected as a beginning step in the reader's response to the text.

In this transaction between reader and text, the reader is actively engaged in thinking about the words on the page; the reader is making meaning from reading literature, meaning that should have an opportunity to be shared and discussed in the classroom. As teachers of literature we must accept the wide range of responses to a text based on the wide range of students' experiences. It is this exchange of responses to literature that often motivates students to become readers.

As teachers we need to remember that the act of reading is first a private experience; each reader uses his or her own personal experience as a bridge or connection to begin to make meaning from a work of literature. If we acknowledge Rosenblatt's transactional theory of reading and agree that reading offers the adolescent an opportunity to test his or her life experiences against the experiences offered in the text, then we must consider seriously Rosenblatt's comment in *Literature as Exploration* (1983) that "choices must reflect a sense of the possible links between these materials and the students' past experience and present level of emotional maturity" (42).

Simply put, we cannot determine what students ought to read without considering their ability to respond to a work of literature on the basis of their personal experiences. What can they relate to in the book? How many teenagers can relate to Arthur Dimmesdale's particular brand of guilt and sin? How many tenth graders can relate to Ethan Frome's acceptance of his stark life caring for Maddie and Zenobia? In what way can a contemporary, urban teenager, possibly raised in a welfare family, relate to Lear's losses? But sometimes a high school student can empathize with Nick's need to leave the East and get away from the Buchanans after Gatsby's death. Or a son who has a difficult parental relationship can understand Biff's shame and disrespect for his father, Willie Loman.

For students who are not ready or who cannot yet respond to Shakespeare, Hemingway, Fitzgerald, James, Wharton, Miller, and other authors of demanding literature, there is a body of quality YAL that invites them to become confident readers, responding readers, and makers of meaning. For example, most seventh or eighth graders from any socioeconomic group can relate to Ponyboy and Sodapop in S. E. Hinton's *The Outsiders*—to their struggle to fit in, their feelings of alienation, seeing perhaps a parallel to Steinbeck's characters George and Lennie in *Of Mice and Men*. Richard Peck's *Remembering the Good Times* describes in compassionate detail the effect of a boy's suicide on his two best friends, something many of today's students can relate to. Many teenage readers can identify with Zoe in Annette Curtis Klause's *The Silver Kiss* as she faces her mother's death from cancer. And other powerful writers such as Sue Ellen Bridgers, Virginia Hamilton, Will Hobbs, Alden Carter, Chris Crutcher, and Jenny Davis provide a compassionate view of teenagers struggling to make sense of a world that tests their perception of morality. As students become makers of meaning in the literature they read, they gain the knowledge to discover and measure their own feelings and beliefs against those of their classmates and to reconsider those opinions and beliefs.

Imagine the act of reading as a series of moments, of words flashing through these moments, stacking up in our memory bank—flashing ideas and images that connect to some event in our past experience, perhaps an event in childhood; we read on and on, weaving a vast mural of these events, and the mural becomes our picture . . . with language it becomes our story. Our students should be weaving their own stories when they respond to a text.

Rosenblatt's theory is important because she validates the reader's personal response as a genuine and authentic beginning in making meaning. The world of the reader is an important component in understanding, enjoying, and respecting literature as a source of knowledge. Rosenblatt reminds us of the possibilities of a literary experience as a social force in the life of the developing reader. She reminds us that the reader's response to the text is not static; as readers mature and wrestle with new ideas and challenges, they are preparing themselves for more insightful transactions with more demanding literature. Rosenblatt uses the phrase "developing social sensitivity"; we might also call it developing a social conscience, a feeling of compassion for the human condition.

Rosenblatt comments: "When the young reader considers why he has responded in a certain way, he is learning both to read more adequately and to seek personal meaning in literature" (*Literature As Exploration*, 70). Perhaps the reader then is moving into what Carlsen calls the philosophical stage; perhaps the reader is moving from an emotional to a cognitive response, independently considering the structure of literature. The more that maturing readers read, the more they begin to recognize patterns in the literature. They begin to connect settings, characters, and plots from other readings. The process continues through personal response as well as through classroom discussion, which can inspire meaningful discussion among readers.

It is during this discussion stage—and it truly must be a discussion, not a question-answer session—that students *share* their individual, personal responses. For example, if several students have read *The Runner* by Cynthia Voigt, they might argue about the father/son relationship, comparing it to their relationship with their own parents. They may question, argue, agree with, or defend their personal feelings about the behavior of particular characters in the novel. They might support or refute a father's right to give orders to a son. They may agree or disagree with each other's responses, going back into the text, reading passages out loud to one another, and at the same time begin to sift out particular details through dialogue and description while reconsidering their responses and interpretations. At this point, students are sharing personal responses as well as discussing literary techniques such as dialogue, character relationships, point of view, and setting. They argue and discuss with conviction, going back into the text to validate opinions. There is no doubt that this kind of student-led discussion provides the most exciting moment in a classroom—it is the essence of why we teach literature.

RESPONSE-BASED TEACHING

Most of us have led our students to the so-called correct meaning of the prescribed literature. And many of us have used published teacher guides, reading aids, packaged quizzes, and tests that encourage a kind of dead-end approach to reading. How do we move away from this comfortable stance and, instead, risk changing to a response-based classroom? It isn't easy.

We need to find a starting point, a comfort zone for our students as well as ourselves. So how do we begin to rethink our time-tested (but time-worn) habits and attitudes about teaching literature? First, you might want to read Carlsen and Rosenblatt to make your own sense of their theories, observations, and conclusions; as readers we should have a personal response to their texts and speculate for ourselves what kinds of changes we need to consider if we want to meet the needs of our students.

As teachers we are suspicious of change, although our students are in a constant state of change. But changing our whole approach to teaching literature can unhinge the most seasoned veteran. And changing from a teacher-centered classroom to a student-centered, response-based classroom is scary. Our students will probably be more open to change than we will.

Fortunately, Robert E. Probst, professor of English at Georgia State University, has written a comprehensive book that encompasses research and application about response-based teaching. In *Response and Analysis: Teaching Literature in Junior and Senior High School* (1988), he explains clearly the nature and structure of response-based teaching as a means of engaging students in their reading of literature. Using Rosenblatt's theory of the transaction between reader and text, Probst describes the reader's response in isolation, the reader's response with other readers, and the reader's relationship with texts. He provides model lessons using reader response, showing how it can be applied in the typical classroom. He demonstrates how reader response engages students in discussion, speculation, and the re-reading of texts, encouraging students to formulate their own knowledge from a text. He emphasizes the importance of reader response in the following statement:

The ideas taught in the literature classroom do not have identity and substance independent of the students; rather, they are produced by the students as they interact with the text. Unless students read and respond, there is no literature to teach—only text and information about texts. (38)

Probst includes an overview of various theories about teaching literature. Because he has observed and taught many literature classes, he describes a variety of strategies by which teachers can engage students in the text and can encourage students to share personal responses.

In Part I, titled "The Logic of Response-Based Teaching," Probst details observations about different kinds of reader response. With clear and concise examples he explains pitfalls, and his suggestions and descriptions focus on a variety of accessible ideas such as response statements, patterns of discussion, the teacher's role, focused writing, variations, pairing texts, and thematic teaching.

In his chapter about adolescent literature (which we are calling Young Adult Literature in this text), Probst explains why Young Adult Literature is important in the teaching of literature; he includes a 26-page bibliography categorized by genre. He agrees with Carlsen and Rosenblatt that students' maturation and development are important considerations in their response to the literature curriculum, particularly a curriculum that is historically based. Probst believes that Young Adult Literature is an important starting point because much of it deals with controversial and contemporary issues that are meaningful to adolescent readers. At the same time, he suggests that YAL can be organized thematically to fit into the standard English curriculum, a procedure we support enthusiastically.

Using Arthur N. Applebee's report entitled *A Study of Book-Length Works Taught in High School English Courses* (1989), we can begin to pair or group some titles from Young Adult Literature with several of the most widely taught traditional titles. Some YAL titles that could be used to tie into *To Kill a Mockingbird*, for example, might include *Notes for Another Life* by Sue Ellen Bridgers, *Up Country* by Alden R. Carter, *Words by Heart* by Ouida Sebestyen, *More Than Meets the Eye* by Jeanne Betancourt, or *Let the Circle Be Unbroken* by Mildred D. Taylor. All deal with family relationships, loneliness, and personal identity.

For *Lord of the Flies*, some novels with common ideas could include *The Chocolate War* by Robert Cormier, *Downriver* by Will Hobbs, *Killing Mr. Griffin* by Lois Duncan, *Princess Ashley* by Richard Peck, or *Scorpions* by Walter Dean Myers. All focus on the conflict between going along with the crowd or being an individual.

Hamlet could be preceded by reading *Maniac Magee* by Jerry Spinelli, *Monkey Island* by Paula Fox, *Running Loose* by Chris Crutcher, *Slake's Limbo* by Felice Holman, or *I Am the Cheese* by Robert Cormier. All deal with young people surviving alone, without parental or adult support, searching for their place in an indifferent society.

The Outsiders by S. E. Hinton, *The Moves Make the Man* by Bruce Brooks, *Sex Education* by Jenny Davis, *Words by Heart* by Ouida Sebestyen, or *The Pigman* by Paul Zindel provide the reader with a view of characters struggling to understand a society interested in self-gratification, a society that exploits its less powerful members, just as Nick, the narrator, does in *The Great Gatsby*. Nick describes Gatsby's need to impress his golden girl, Daisy Buchanan, at any cost. Yet Nick is overwhelmed by Tom Buchanan's treatment of Mabel and Daisy's indifference to Gatsby's death. The YAL novels are good starting points before reading *Gatsby* because they, too, present main characters in situations that reflect the cruelty and selfish behaviors of dispassionate people.

Many of these novels can be bridged by theme, setting, character predicaments, and other common threads. Our next chapter will include many more examples of grouping Young Adult Literature with traditional titles from the literary canon.

Probst's most provocative remark as to why we should include adolescent literature in response-based teaching is: "Literature courses conceived as repositories of the great works are likely to be more like a walk through a graveyard than an encounter with the minds of great writers and thinkers" (1988, 205). Our best way to avoid the graveyard is to read and discuss the myriad ways in which we can use Young Adult Literature as an entry into the classics and/or contemporary literature in the standard English curriculum.

Chapter 4

BUILDING BRIDGES: GETTING STUDENTS FROM WHEREVER THEY ARE TO WHERE THE CURRICULUM SAYS THEY SHOULD BE

On a recent Sunday evening, a friend who teaches high school English in another town telephoned me in panic. She was teaching a course in American literature to an average level class, who, for the most part, were nonreaders. Her previous literature unit had been a failure; she was starting *The Scarlet Letter* the next day. She remembered my discussion about using YAL as a bridge to the classics, and she wondered if I had any ideas. Fortunately, I had just written down some rough ideas about common themes between YAL and *The Scarlet Letter*, so I read them to her, suggesting some YAL titles. She must have a very cooperative school librarian, because she called later in the week to tell me that the librarian had pulled the titles from the shelves, the students were reading the YA novels, and by the following week they were planning to write essays about some of the common themes in their YA novels and *The Scarlet Letter*. She felt that the YA novels paved the way for stronger discussion and writing about Hawthorne's classic novel.

Please understand that I am not advocating this example as a way to test the viability of YA novels to introduce a classic; I relate this anecdote to remind you that all of us at one time or another find ourselves in desperate circumstances. But don't wait until you are in such a desperate circumstance to try YAL in your classroom. Rather, if you use it on a regular basis and you and your students enjoy it together, the connection will already be there.

By linking YAL with the classics, we can see our students become developing readers, connecting, comparing, and drawing parallels about

the elements of literature they discover independently. By using both the
suggested YA titles and the traditional titles from the literary canon, we
can help our students begin to realize the delight and power of literature.

BEING FLEXIBLE

It is not necessary to have full class sets of each title. Rather, try five
or more copies of several different titles on the same theme. Or try
grouping titles according to plot, characterization, setting, style, or historical period, depending on the traditional title you are planning to teach to
the whole class. By offering students a choice of titles, you are encouraging
them to begin to own their reading; that is, you are allowing them to take
responsibility for reading and discovering the connections between their
YA title and the class text. And, if the class is grouped according to title
selection, students enjoy meeting with others in their group and comparing responses to the book. (Discussions might be more productive if
students have been assigned to keep reading logs or response journals.)
After the whole class has read and/or discussed the assigned classic,
students can regroup by YA title to exchange critical opinions and interpretations about both books: e.g., focusing on common theme(s), character motivations, or literary techniques. Because this is student-directed,
the teacher, rather than providing restrictive guide questions, should be
eavesdropping among student groups, listening to students' opinions, and
acting as a coach/provocateur by joining in when necessary.

Reading the YA titles, before or after reading the classic, helps students
become confident, independent readers. Based on my own classroom
experience, this type of freedom in reading choices encourages readers of
various abilities to become engaged and enthusiastic in their responses to
literature. And the titles in the required literary canon do not seem as
intimidating to less motivated readers, because YA titles, in most instances, help them to begin to feel confident about making connections
between and drawing inferences from different works of literature.

This approach also affords you the opportunity to integrate multicultural books and books about women into the otherwise white Eurocentric
curriculum. Instead of introducing a work of literature as, for example, a
book about African Americans, you might introduce it as a story about
the importance of family, or taking a moral stand, or a journey of
self-discovery. We have included many such titles throughout this text.
All multicultural titles are identified in the bibliography with an asterisk
(*). We will use the asterisk for the same purpose in subsequent pages in
this chapter.

As you use YAL more and more in your classroom and listen to students'
responses, you will learn which books "work" and which don't. As you
read more and more YAL, you will find that your choices sometimes do

and sometimes don't coincide with the students' choices; but the wider the variety of titles, and the more the students participate and suggest titles, the more motivated readers you will have in your classroom. Sometimes you must keep silent, because you'll disagree and consider some student responses "way out" or a "ridiculous stretch of the imagination." But remember, your students are reading, responding, and sharing opinions and ideas with authority.

You will not feel ignored in this classroom; you will feel that you have transmitted your enthusiasm for reading and literature. Many students will take pride in reading and many will become more confident readers. The tone of the class will change, too—it is exciting to see students take command of their learning and to respect reading and discussing literature.

Your new role in the classroom eliminates the need for the usual question-and-answer period to see who read the assignment. It's no longer necessary to prepare chapter-by-chapter quizzes or tests to check on assigned reading; students' commitment to their reading group is motivation enough to come to class prepared. Instead, you can move about the classroom listening, or you can join a different group each period as a participant. You will be hearing responses from those students who were too shy to speak in front of the whole class, as well as those students who were often unprepared. You can check on students' reading by assigning reading logs, double-entry reading journals, or response questions or essays. But most important, you are cultivating positive reading habits in students—habits that we hope will remain with them throughout their lifetime.

The best advice I can offer is to be very flexible about allowing students to choose their books and to allow lots of time for reading, for small-group discussion, and for changes in students' reading attitudes. At the risk of sounding audacious, I would say allow two weeks; and if you are willing to take a risk, let the student groups determine how many pages they will read each week and how many periods they will need to discuss their title. Some of my students finish their book in two weeks or less. Being in charge or in control of their reading assignment instills a sense of self-esteem, trust, and responsibility in most students. Believe in your students and let them know you listen to and welcome their responses, ideas, and opinions about their reading. My most amazing discovery in working with YAL along with classic or traditional literature is the feeling of inclusiveness—all kinds and levels of readers are not frightened or embarrassed to participate in class. It has been my experience that when one title is read, usually the same few students do all the talking; but when multiple titles are read and discussed, everyone participates in his or her group.

MAKING CONNECTIONS

Let's consider some YAL that connects with the traditional titles required in most English programs. *Remember: titles that deal with multicultural themes or issues are followed by an asterisk (*).*

——————————— / / / ———————————

*The Adventures of Huckleberry Finn** by Mark Twain

Themes

1. innocent's initiation into the evil world
2. journey to find self
3. finding harmony and peace in nature as opposed to "civilized society"
4. surviving in an intolerant and prejudiced society
5. coming-of-age among charlatans, liars, cheaters
6. surviving without adult role models

Suggested YAL titles that share some of these key themes:

CORMIER, ROBERT. *Tunes for Bears to Dance to.*

After his brother dies, Henry's parents ignore him. Because his father is depressed and unable to work, Henry gets a job in a local grocery store. The owner, Mr. Hairston, reveals his prejudices about people in the neighborhood, using racial and ethnic epithets. Henry becomes fascinated by an older man, follows him to a community craft center, and watches him make an exquisite wood carving of the village he left behind during the Holocaust. Henry makes the mistake of sharing this information with his boss, who threatens to fire Henry unless he breaks into the craft center and destroys the old man's wood carving, which is going to be displayed in the mayor's office. Mr. Hairston is a fully developed evil character who exploits Henry's need to help support his family. If Henry will destroy the wood carving, Mr. Hairston will give him money for a gravestone for his brother's grave, and other gifts. Henry cannot discuss this moral choice with his parents; weighing the "gifts" he will be able to offer his family, he performs the evil deed. But his conscience will not allow him to forget. He refuses Mr. Hairston's rewards and returns to help the old man rebuild his model village.

Theme Connector

Like Huck, Henry is alienated from family; he has no adults to guide him. When confronted with evil in the form of Mr. Hairston, Henry obeys him. But Henry leaves his job of his own volition when he realizes the significance of his destructive deed. Huck is not alone. With Jim, a runaway slave, he travels the river seeking a place where he can be accepted as he is. But Huck's journey on the river presents many challenges. Like Henry, he meets up with evil men, the Duke and the King, who are charlatans. Huck gains knowledge about slavery and makes a moral choice to help Jim escape. Although Henry and Huck are consciously exploited by adults in both novels, they learn to trust adults who have a sense of morality.

CRUTCHER, CHRIS. *The Crazy Horse Electric Game.**

When Willie, a top athlete in Coho, Montana, has a waterskiing accident that at first paralyzes him and later impairs his coordination and gait, his friends tolerate him but he has to live life from a very different perspective. And his father, a former athletic hero, is ashamed of him. When the situation becomes unbearable, Willie gets on a bus and runs away to Oakland, California. He lives in the ghetto and attends a "last chance" high school where a gym teacher helps him to exercise and rebuild his body. Although Willie does not regain his former athletic ability, he does gain knowledge about his inner strengths. He learns to appreciate his mind and his ability to concentrate, and most of all, to appreciate the kindness and acceptance of the people in this very different community. He returns to Montana, a whole person; but his parents are no longer together. His family now becomes the people in the ghetto fighting for a better life.

Theme Connector

Willie and Huck are two adolescents who witness the inhumane behavior of individuals against the uneducated, the disabled, and the poor, and begin to understand intolerance. When Willie feels he is no longer accepted by his father or friends and leaves home, he is alone, like Huck, trying to find his way. Ironically, both meet up with black men who help them: Willie meets a pimp, Lacey, who gives him shelter and food; Huck travels with Jim, a runaway slave. Both adults offer Willie and Huck protection, which helps them gain knowledge and wisdom through these experiences.

PAULSEN, GARY. *Hatchet* and *The River*.

Brian Robeson, the protagonist in both these short novels, survives in the Canadian wilderness in *Hatchet* and saves a pyschologist's life in the sequel, *The River*. Both stories are about Brian using his inner resources to survive in the wilderness and to meet the physical and mental challenges in human relationships. By the end of these novels Brian has learned to take responsibility for his life. He has also learned that he is capable of surviving his parents' divorce.

Theme Connector

Hatchet reveals Brian's ingenuity and perseverance, while *The River* reveals Brian's capacity to cope under the worst physical circumstances. Brian survives without adults in both cases; like Huck, he goes through profound changes that help him become an independent person. Brian builds a raft, and his journey on the river is dangerous; he has to use his innermost physical and mental strength to survive. Both Brian and Huck learn how to take care of themselves in demanding circumstances. Their river journey enables them to test their survival skills.

Some other YAL titles to mesh with themes in *Huckleberry Finn* include:

Armstrong, William. *Sounder.** A young boy learns about prejudice when his father is put in jail.

Avi. *The True Confessions of Charlotte Doyle.** Charlotte's journey to Providence changes her view of life when she meets the evil Captain Jaggery.

Block, Francesca Lia. *Weetzie Bat.** Weetzie establishes her California lifestyle without parents.

Bridgers, Sue Ellen. *Permanent Connections*. Rob's rebellion is subverted when he connects to his family in North Carolina.

Carter, Alden. *Up Country*. When he has to go "up country," Carl learns about family.

Cormier, Robert. *The Chocolate War*. Jerry Renault tries to find himself in an evil world.

Covington, Dennis. *Lizard.** Experiencing intolerance because of his scarred face, Lizard runs away to find acceptance and respect.

Crutcher, Chris. *Chinese Handcuffs*. Dillon learns about protecting himself in an evil world.

———. *Staying Fat for Sarah Byrnes*. Eric exemplifies the true meaning of friendship as he remains loyal to the emotionally and physically scarred Sarah Byrnes.

Paterson, Katherine. *Lyddie*. Lyddie exhibits strength and courage in a society that constantly tries to exploit her.

Paulsen, Gary. *The Island*. Will finds himself while living on an island and writing in a journal about watching, listening to, knowing, and understanding nature's creatures that surround him.

Wolff, Virginia Euwer. *Make Lemonade.** LaVaughn helps an unwed mother, Jolly, survive in an indifferent society.

Note: Huckleberry Finn appears frequently on censorship lists in various school districts. An interesting novel to introduce the *Huckleberry Finn* censorship dilemma is Nat Hentoff's *The Day They Came to Arrest the Book.** In this story the new librarian, Ms. Fitzgerald, and a history teacher, Ms. Baines, confront the school principal when he listens to parental requests to ban *The Adventures of Huckleberry Finn* from the school library. The principal ignores the policy of the review committee because he is willing to bow to political pressure. The novel presents the point of view of students, parents, and faculty members regarding the censorship of books in school classrooms and the library.

——————————————— / / / ———————————————

The Grapes of Wrath by John Steinbeck

Themes

1. denial of the American Dream
2. exclusion from the American mainstream
3. importance of family and home
4. displaced people
5. exploitation of poor people

Suggested YAL titles that share some of these key themes:

BRIDGERS, SUE ELLEN. *Home before Dark.*
Fourteen-year-old Stella Mae Wilson and her family have never lived in a house. As migrant workers, they travel around harvesting crops, carrying all their belongings in a station wagon. When Stella Mae's father decides to return to his family's farm in Ohio and settle down, her mother, Mae, panics. The experience of living in a permanent place awes Stella Mae; she adapts easily, finding pleasure in living near a small Ohio town. But her mother, who is a second-generation migrant worker, cannot adapt to this permanent home. While harvesting tobacco, the mother is accidentally killed in an electrical storm. The father decides to move the family into town, but Stella Mae refuses to leave the cottage, fearing they will become migrant workers again.

Theme Connector

Through well-developed characters, both novels show the importance of a sense of place, or "putting down roots," to family life. The Joads and the Wilsons share some of the experiences of migrant workers—a sense of unconnectedness and the harsh living conditions. However, Stella Mae and her family have spent many years following the harvesting of crops by their own choice. They have never had a permanent home. To Stella Mae, the station wagon carrying them from farm to farm is a sort of home. But the Joads, because of the Oklahoma dust storms and the bank foreclosures, are *forced* to leave their permanent home to become migrant workers. They travel to California, seeking a permanent place to begin again; but they are exploited by the growers and shunned by the California authorities. They are not allowed to find a new place in California; they become displaced people.

Both novels use strong characters to illustrate the injustices that become part of their daily experience. And both novels examine the psychological effects of poverty on migrant families. Although Stella Mae's family does find roots when they return to her father's birthplace, they are passive and accepting of her uncle's and aunt's decisions about their lives. Although the Joads maintain their sense of dignity under horrible circumstances, they too have been beaten down by a system that excludes them from the American Dream.

SPINELLI, JERRY. *Maniac Magee.**

When his parents die, Maniac runs away from a cruel uncle and aunt. Wandering around a city of working-class people, Maniac is a modern-day Candide, buffeted by racism and prejudice, withstanding all sorts of human cruelty. Because he is an innocent, Maniac does not understand prejudice; he is unable to react to the cruelties inflicted by people, both black and white. Maniac's journey exposes the indifference of society to homeless people; the lack of compassion and understanding for Maniac is ironic.

Theme Connector

Maniac's search for a home and family parallels the Joads' search for roots with their large family. The dignity of Maniac and the Joads is reflected in many situations in both novels. The Joads' willingness to share and to help others in need when they have so little is touching. Maniac is grateful and accepting in his interaction with both white and black people, yet only one family—a black family—tries to adopt Maniac.

Both novels expose the need for compassion among human beings and the need to share our resources with one another, rather than fulfilling self. *Maniac Magee* appears to be a simple novel, but it reveals a cross-section of Americans who are compassionate and caring, and others who are insensitive and violent.

PECK, ROBERT NEWTON. *Arly.**

Set in rural Florida in 1927, this novel tells the story of 11-year-old Arly and his father, Dan Poole, a produce picker. They live in Shack Row in Jailtown, a company town controlled by Captain Tant, who owns the store, the sugar mill, the crops, and, essentially, the pickers and their families. The pickers and their families are treated brutally by the field boss. Arly is just about to be assigned to a job in the sugar mill when a schoolteacher, Miss Hoe, arrives in Jailtown. Arly's father enrolls Arly in school so that he can learn to read and write and better himself. Arly is innately bright, and Miss Hoe encourages Arly to read and learn. The field boss tries to assign Arly to the fields after his father's death, but Miss Hoe rescues Arly from Shack Row and arranges for him to leave Jailtown. The novel includes many details of the sunup-to-sundown work life of pickers and their families. Arly's intelligence and loyalty to his father's memory, along with Miss Hoe's support, help him to escape the oppression of Shack Row.

PECK, ROBERT NEWTON. *Arly's Run.**

With his teacher's help, Arly is on his way to Moore Haven, Florida, to go to school and live with a family. He can hear the field boss and the dogs trying to pick up his scent as he sits with Brother Smith in a sculler on Lake Okeechobee. During the journey on the lake the sculler capsizes and Arly floats toward a light on shore. However, a field boss and his assistant meet him with mean, vicious coon dogs. They are convinced Arly is a runaway picker, so they burn numbers onto his chest and throw him inside a shack to await the pickup bus. Soon Arly finds himself a picker from dawn to dusk, like his father once was. He befriends an old man, Coo Coo, and they comfort one another under the most dehumanized conditions. The workers sleep in old, battered buses that carry them from farms to groves, picking crops. At times Arly wants to give up and die. Eventually he uses his ingenuity to escape with Coo Coo, but not for long. When a hurricane hits Florida, Arly's hope of finding the family in Moore Haven dies. He is reunited with Miss Hoe and they return to rebuild a new Jailtown—a new community with schools, homes, and decent wages for the pickers.

Theme Connector

Arly, Arly's Run, and *The Grapes of Wrath* reflect the theme of exclusion or denial of the American Dream as well as exploitation of poor people. Readers can compare the treatment of migrant workers in Florida and California: wages go directly to the company store, where the workers are overcharged for food, kerosene, clothing, and rent for shacks. The living conditions are so squalid that family members die from typhoid fever because of the lack of clean drinking water; others die of starvation. Young children are expected to work in the fields all day long for half-wages. Because migrant workers are not residents of any towns or areas, they are disenfranchised from mainstream society—they do not vote, their children do not attend public schools. The Joads move around with more freedom than the Pooles, but they do not have a better life. The love and loyalty between Arly and his father and among the Joads is poignant. The field bosses of the orchards, groves, and farms—who are white men—treat the Pooles and the Joads with contempt and disdain. Despite the most trying and inhumane conditions, these American families manage to maintain their sense of pride and dignity.

Other YAL titles that focus on similar themes about the search for the American Dream and the importance of family are:

Davis, Jenny. *Checking on the Moon*. Cab spends the summer with her grandmother in Washco and finds out about urban neighborhoods.

Hamilton, Virginia. *Sweet Whispers, Brother Rush*.* Tree Sweet and her retarded brother live together in an apartment while their mother works.

Myers, Walter Dean. *Somewhere in the Darkness*.* Jimmy Little and his father, Crab, go on a journey to learn about each other.

Paterson, Katherine. *Lyddie*. Lyddie survives the mills in Lowell, Massachusetts, and reunites the family.

Paulsen, Gary. *Nightjohn*.* Twelve-year-old Sarny describes Nightjohn's underground school for slaves and the white owners' punishments.

Taylor, Mildred. *Let the Circle Be Unbroken*.* A story about a courageous family that struggles to combat prejudice and poverty.

Voigt, Cynthia. *Homecoming*.* Dicey overcomes many challenges as she keeps her family together.

Wolff, Virginia Euwer. *Make Lemonade*.* Fourteen-year-old LaVaughn helps Jolly, an unwed mother of two toddlers, learn to become a responsible mother and student.

--------------------------------------- / / / ---------------------------------------

Great Expectations by Charles Dickens

Themes

1. the value of loyal and trustworthy friends
2. the illusion that money brings happiness
3. the influence of wealth on class structure
4. the search for one's place in society

Suggested YAL titles that share some of these key themes:

PULLMAN, PHILIP. *Ruby in the Smoke*.
In 1872 in Victorian London, 16-year-old Sally Lockhart investigates her father's death. She visits the shipping firm he owned with a partner, Mr. Selby. She is referred to a Mr. Higgs; and when she questions him about the phrase "the Seven Blessings," he gasps and dies. So starts Sally's intense investigation of her father's past. Without any parents, Sally is placed in the care of a distant cousin, Miss Rees, who is indifferent and cruel to her. In the course of trying to unravel the mystery of her father's

death on a ship out of Singapore, Sally comes into contact with seedy and life-threatening characters—such as the evil Mrs. Holland, who is out to kill Sally for the Ruby of Agrapur; and Hendrik Van Eden, alias Ah Ling. With the help of her new friends—the photographer Frederick Garland, his sister Rosa, and a young clerk named Jim—she uncovers more and more details about the ruby and her father's "accidental" death. Sally is a well-developed character who consistently demonstrates tenacity, intelligence, and independence. By the end of the novel she solves her father's murder, finds her inheritance, and establishes a family relationship with Frederick, Rosa, and Jim.

Theme Connector

The setting of both *Ruby in the Smoke* and *Great Expectations* offers striking images of Victorian London. Although *Ruby in the Smoke* uses more mystery and suspense, Pullman's images of London with coaches clattering on foggy, cobblestone streets, along with dark alleys and isolated wharves on the river, are reminiscent of Dickens's London. Both authors place the orphaned main characters in challenging situations with sinister, deceitful people. Adelaide, an orphan who is terrified of the unmerciful Mrs. Holland, conjures up images of Dickensian mudlarks along the waterfronts of London.

Both Sally and Pip share common experiences as they seek their true identity; during the course of their journey their systems of honesty, trust, and fairness are tested again and again. As they grow and develop from these experiences, they learn the truth about themselves and their families. Sally learns that Mr. Marchbanks, her real father, was an opium addict who in a blind moment gave her to Lockhart in exchange for the ruby. Pip learns that his benefactor was a convict, not the class-conscious Miss Havisham. His infatuation with Estella is manipulated cruelly by Miss Havisham; but when he returns from his experiences trying to be a London gentleman, he begins to appreciate the value of love, friendship, and loyalty offered by his country friends Biddy and Joe. Sally becomes wary of most people after her experiences with her guardian, Miss Rees; the opium dealer Ah Ling; and her father's partner, Mr. Selby. But by the end of the novel she realizes that Frederick, Rosa, and Jim are her loyal friends. Both Pip and Sally share similar traits such as loyalty, honesty, and commitment.

PULLMAN, PHILIP. *Shadow in the North*.

In the sequel to *Ruby in the Smoke*, Sally Lockhart is 22 years old and an established financial consultant in London. When one of her clients, a retired teacher, complains to Sally about her financial loss in the Anglo Baltic Company, Sally begins an investigation with her close friends, the photographer Frederick Garland and the private detective Jim Taylor. She finds that the financier Axel Bellmann is selling armaments and is developing a destructive weapon called the Steam Gun. He has managed, through subterfuge, to buy a rail car manufacturing company, dismiss many workers, and set up a secret manufacturing operation, causing high unemployment and widespread poverty among the working classes. Bellmann tries to become socially prominent by marrying the daughter of a well-known family. When he realizes that Sally and Frederick are learning too much about him, he arranges for their home to be set on fire. While trying to rescue a friend staying at their home, Frederick is killed in the fire. Sally, having realized that she trusted and loved Frederick, is devastated by his death and is determined to avenge it. By the end of the novel, Sally, Frederick's uncle Webster, and Jim have moved outside London to start over. When Charles Bertram, Frederick's friend, gives Sally the only known portrait of Frederick, she shares her secret that she is pregnant with Frederick's child. His uncle Webster, Jim, and Rosa have become her close family.

Theme Connector

In this novel, Sally's sense of right and wrong is tested again. She contends with the evil Axel Bellmann and with courage and conviction she exposes his ruthless attempt to destroy the trade unions that were developing at the time. Both Sally and Pip learn to use their inner resources to cope with ruthless people: Pip has to deal with Miss Havisham and her warped sense of a romantic relationship, and Sally has to expose Axel Bellmann's duplicity. Both novels contrast in vivid detail the lives of the rich upper class and the horrible living conditions of the poor.

PULLMAN, PHILIP. *The Tiger in the Well.*

The year is 1881 and Sally Lockhart, mother of a 21-month-old daughter, Harriet, is comfortably established in Orchard House outside of London. However, a man arrives with a legal document suing Sally for divorce and custody of her daughter. The man, Arthur Parrish, is unknown to Harriet; before she can respond, she has lost her bank accounts, home, and business because of the Property Laws. Sally leaves with Harriet and wanders from place to place, finally staying in a women's shelter. Under an assumed identity she exposes a sinister business run by Mr. Parrish's employer: young, penniless females who are escaping from the pogroms of Eastern Europe sign contracts for employment with the mysterious Zaddik, who exploits them as prostitutes. Sally does not know who is after her or why, but she eventually unravels the motives for revenge and meets up with an old enemy. While living in the women's shelter, Sally is an eyewitness to the squalid living conditions of poor people. She visits sweatshops and rented rooms in courtyards where the sewage overflows into the streets.

She also meets a new group of people who help her to change her interest in being a successful businesswoman. Instead, she develops a strong social conscience and is determined to help the poor and the immigrants to have access to better health care, housing, and education.

Theme Connector

In this third novel of Pullman's trilogy, Sally appears to be defenseless. The justice system has taken away her property and security; she is wanted by the police because of the custody suit. She is bewildered, frightened, and hopeless. She finds a place at a women's shelter among women she can trust. She also experiences firsthand the poverty, despair, and hopelessness of poor people in London. When she sees their living conditions, she is shocked. She realizes that her former upper-class life was hypocritical, and by the end of the novel she is committed to closing the gap between the rich and the poor. Similarly, Pip returns to his humble surroundings with his dear friends, Joe and Biddy, and has changed his attitude about simple, country people. Through their disappointments and challenges, both Pip and Sally have learned to appreciate the value of loyal friends.

AVI. *The True Confessions of Charlotte Doyle.* *

In 1832, a 13-year-old proper young lady, Miss Charlotte Doyle, is traveling from Liverpool, England, to Providence, Rhode Island, to rejoin her family. Her father has booked passage for her on one of his company's ships, the *Seahawk.* Although Charlotte is alarmed that she is the only passenger, she starts out on the journey. When one of the crew members, Zachariah, tries to befriend her, she rebuffs him because he is a Negro and is beneath her social station. With her white gloves and her desire to associate only with Captain Jaggery, Charlotte reveals her snobbery to the crew. Although Zachariah helps her when she falls ill and warns her about Jaggery's evil disposition, she refuses to believe him. Finally, however, she witnesses Jaggery's cruel behavior. When she confronts Jaggery, he ignores her. The crew refuses to accept her because she has betrayed them. But after proving herself, she becomes a crew member and moves to their quarters, where she learns about trust, loyalty, and friendship. Jaggery tries her for murder; when he attempts to kill her, Zachariah saves her life. After the voyage she returns home to her family but finds their upper-class snobbery intolerable; she returns to the *Seahawk* to be with her loving friends, especially Zachariah.

Theme Connector

Through a painful journey, both Charlotte and Pip discover the truth about upper-class society. Pip is mercilessly ridiculed by so-called gentlemen and the beautiful ward of Miss Havisham, Estella, until he realizes that Biddy and Joe are true friends who love him as he is. Charlotte has attended private school and presumes that her family's position in society makes her superior to the crew members. However, when she witnesses the cruelty and violence of Jaggery against the crew, she begins to realize his evil nature. When she returns to her family and tries to share what she has learned from her journey on the *Seahawk*, they reject her explanations and accuse her of an overly active imagination. Because she cannot tolerate their attitude and snobbishness, she leaves home and returns to her new family—Zachariah and the crew.

Other YAL titles that tie into these themes are:

Buss, Fran Leeper. *Journey of the Sparrows.** Fourteen-year-old Maria and her sisters are El Salvadoran refugees trying to survive in Chicago without a green card.

David, Terry. *If Rock and Roll Were a Machine*. Bert Bowden's journey on his Harley-Davidson helps him find himself.

Guy, Rosa. *The Friends.** Phyllisia respects Edith's attempt to take care of her four sisters alone.

Mahy, Margaret. *Memory*. When Johnny Dart meets the "bag lady" Sophie, she changes the course of his life.

Mazer, Norma Fox. *Silver*. Although she lives in a trailer camp, Silver learns that she and her mother enjoy a loving relationship envied by her well-to-do new friends.

Peck, Richard. *Unfinished Portrait of Jessica*. After a disastrous visit with her father in Mexico, Jessica discovers her mother's love and understanding.

Wolff, Virginia Euwer. *Make Lemonade.** LaVaughn babysits for Jolly, a 17-year-old unwed mother with two young children; she helps Jolly reconnect with society.

----- / / / -----

The Great Gatsby by F. Scott Fitzgerald

Themes

1. initiation into an amoral society
2. the need to compromise in order to survive
3. the excesses of "winning at all costs"
4. the acceptance of amoral behavior as the norm
5. testing one's sense of morality; making a moral choice
6. denial of the American Dream

Suggested YAL titles that share some of these key themes:

CRUTCHER, CHRIS. *Running Loose.* *

Louie Banks, a senior in high school, is the narrator of this coming-of-age story. Like most adolescents, Louie is involved in sports, with a peer group, and with a special girlfriend, Becky. As narrator, Louie tells his story about the unraveling of his world and how he manages to survive. Louie "plays by the rules"—he has a strong sense of morality—but he learns that some adults in society are corrupt and self-serving. In order to win an important football game, the coach tells the team to deliberately injure the star of the opponents' team. When the star player is carried off on a stretcher, Louie decides to take a moral stand and report the coach to the referee. Louie's moral choice alienates him from his peers as well as from the coach and the school principal. Because he chooses not to compromise his values, Louie cannot find a comfortable place within his community. When Becky, his only confidante and friend, dies, he is shattered. The last pages of the novel are riveting—Louie shares "what I have learned," the knowledge he has gained about surviving in a corrupt world.

Theme Connector

Although Louie is a teenager and Nick, the narrator of *The Great Gatsby*, is an Ivy League graduate working on Wall Street, they share naive views of adult behaviors and relationships. When they encounter amoral people—in Nick's case, Daisy, Tom Buchanan, and Jordan Baker; in Louie's case, the football coach, school principal, and members of the football team—the reader can almost feel Nick and Louie reeling. Both Nick and Louie share some solid values (honesty, fair play, loyalty, trust), and when these values are tested as they interact with other characters, they are confused and repelled by the indifference of those characters. They go through a transformation: Nick must leave the East and "cleanse" himself in the Midwest; Louie will continue to stand up for what he believes in at all costs, because ultimately he has to live with himself.

The novels share some common techniques: a strong first person narrator, flashbacks, secondary characters who demonstrate guile and deceit without remorse, and lots of dialogue between the protagonists and antagonists as well as introspective comments. Nick and Louie's voices are vibrant and realistic as they draw the reader into their shock and disgust with other characters' behavior.

LOWRY, LOIS. *The Giver.*

Twelve-year-old Jonas lives in a futuristic community where all of society's ills, such as lies, deceit, disrespect, and disease are under control. Also controlled are sexual awakening, memory, and emotion. No one in this controlled society can experience the feeling of love; no one has experienced snow, colors, or flowers; only black and white exist,

literally and figuratively. By the time children reach the age of 12 they
are assigned their lifetime jobs in the community by the Committee of
Elders, based on their performance from birth to 12 years of age. As Jonas
sits in the auditorium waiting with his classmates, he is the last student
assigned. To his surprise, he is assigned Receiver of Memory, the most
prestigious job in the community! His life changes dramatically as he
attends daily meetings with the aged Receiver of Memory, who now calls
himself The Giver. Slowly The Giver introduces Jonas to colors, flowers,
snow, and other beautiful wonders of the world; however, he also has to
give horrible memories to Jonas, such as death, disease, suffering,
intolerance, and cruelty. As Jonas absorbs the intense evil and ugliness,
he becomes sensitized to the horrors in his community. For example, he
learns that "to be released" means to be killed. His father, who works at
the Nurturing Center, brings home a young baby, Gabriel, who is not
sleeping well, cries a lot, and is developing too slowly. Even though
Jonas's family has the permissible number of family members—mother,
father, sister, brother—his father has permission to try to help Gabriel.
Jonas helps Gabriel sleep through the night by transmitting some pleas-
ant, beautiful memories that The Giver has shared with him. Because
The Giver has access to all procedures, decisions, and actions in the
community, Jonas sees his own father kill a young baby by injection.
Because Jonas's training allows him to experience pain, sorrow, and
compassion, and because he is developing a sense of morality outside of
the community's rules and values, he is tortured by what he begins to
realize about his community. When his father decides that the baby
Gabriel must be returned to the Nurturing Center, Jonas shares his
concern with The Giver, who supports Jonas's decision to leave the
community and to save Gabriel as well.

Theme Connector

Although *The Giver* has a futuristic setting, the community is as callous
and indifferent as Daisy, Tom Buchanan, and Jordan Baker are in *The
Great Gatsby*. Nick and Jonas share similar character traits: compassion,
honesty, caring, loyalty, and trust. The plots of the novels peel away an
amoral world; Nick and Jonas have to interact with characters who refuse
to acknowledge their amoral acts. Of course, in Jonas's community, the
adults and young people take drugs to suppress their emotions so that
they do not confront any sense of morality. But in a sense, the characters
in *The Great Gatsby* also use a drug—bootleg alcohol—to suppress their
sense of right and wrong. Both protagonists leave the community when
their consciences will not allow them to tolerate the moral corruption.
Jonas plots his escape in order to force his community to change, while
Nick leaves the east to "cleanse" himself after Gatsby's death. Jonas and

Nick realize the pain and pleasure of the truth and make a moral choice to remove themselves from intolerable circumstances.

The denial of the American Dream could be included in studying *The Giver* also, because Jonas's training sessions as the Receiver of Memory have made him realize the value of each individual's life. Nick cannot tolerate the Buchanans' indifference to the deaths of Gatsby and Mabel. Although he realizes that Gatsby's fantasy and obsession with Daisy are distorted, he feels compassion for Gatsby as a human being.

Other YAL novels that share some of these themes are:

Cole, Brock. *Celine*. A young adolescent learns to compromise a family situation and strengthen her sense of self.

Davis, Jenny. *Checking on the Moon*. Living with her grandmother in an urban area sharpens Cab's sense of responsibility.

Greene, Bette. *The Drowning of Stephan Jones*. Carla has to choose between romance and her conscience when she witnesses cruel and unjust actions.

Murrow, Liza Ketchum. *Twelve Days in August*.* Todd O'Connor has to make a moral choice when his teammates reveal their homophobia.

Peck, Richard. *Unfinished Portrait of Jessica*. In searching for her father's love, Jessica finds his amoral behavior unacceptable.

———————————————— / / / ————————————————

Hamlet by William Shakespeare

Themes

1. initiation of the innocent into an evil world
2. dealing with loss of a parent
3. abandoning one's sense of morality to seek revenge
4. risking one's place in the community to take a stand
5. surviving without parental support

Suggested YAL titles that share some of these key themes:

BROOKS, BRUCE. *What Hearts*.

This third person narrative is about Asa, a precocious, proud, and perceptive boy who learns at an early age to appear rational despite the continuous upheavals in his life. In the first part, six-year-old Asa eagerly runs home on the last day of school to share his excellent report card and awards with his parents. However, the house is empty and his mother announces that she and his father are divorcing. Asa is confused and disappointed, but he says nothing to her about his report card and awards; he doesn't question or react. He calmly packs up his things. Asa's behavior is odd, unusual, strange from a psychological point of view. He does not react when his mother tells him that she is reuniting with Dave, a former boyfriend. Within a few weeks, Asa realizes that Dave is mean and that it's okay to hate him. Asa's insight and "bead" on his life are shared with the reader; his interaction with other people is calculated; his interior analysis of all aspects of his life is so precise that it is difficult to believe he is a child. As he grows older, Asa's insight and intelligence make him seem different and "scary" to his peers. There are incidents with his mother, friends at school, teachers, and Dave that make him an enigma.

When Asa is in seventh grade, a girl in his class named Jean says, "You figure things out and you attack." She explains to him that she means he knows how to *get* to people. For the first time in his life, Asa connects to another human being and feels attracted to this girl. In his usual analytical manner, he tries to learn how love is supposed to feel. He listens to music but still can't figure out what he is supposed to feel. Finally he asks his mother, who explains her feelings. But in explaining love to Asa, she realizes that she is not in love with Dave and decides to divorce him and move away. Asa tells Jean that he loves her, and she returns her love with candy hearts that say "I love you." When Asa calls Jean to say goodbye, he reaches out for the first time in his life and thanks her for the hearts. She responds, "What hearts?" Asa is canny enough to realize at that moment that his love meant nothing to Jean; and Asa, who is always in control, will not allow himself to feel any disappointment. He thinks to himself, "And if a fellow had *these* words . . . then surely something was in store in the future."

Theme Connector

Although Asa is much younger than Hamlet, they share certain common circumstances. Both are without a father, although Hamlet speaks to his father's ghost. Both have mothers who are so indifferent and self-centered that they neglect the emotional development of their sons. Gertrude doesn't help Hamlet when he is mourning his father's death. Asa's mother doesn't ask Asa about his feelings when she decides to divorce his father; she doesn't offer any emotional support during her marriage to Dave, even though they move approximately ten times. Hamlet's mother expects him to accept her marriage to his Uncle Claudius; she treats his mourning for his father's death lightly. Both mothers do not seem to know their sons; both ignore their emotional needs.

Ironically, Asa and Hamlet also share some common character traits— they are masters at pretense. Their public and private personae intimidate their stepfathers, their mothers, and their friends. Although they sometimes exhibit passive behavior, there is a dark side to their nature that is capable of evil schemes. Because Asa has been neglected by most adults throughout his life, he is independent and reflective and can share his perceptions about the evil he sees in his school and home life. Unlike

Hamlet, however, he does not have to sacrifice himself to gain revenge against his mother or Dave. Hamlet, through his soliloquies, shares the depth of his anguish about his father's unnatural death in the infested kingdom and forces himself to seek revenge. Perhaps Asa will survive because he is prepared to take care of himself; in contrast, Hamlet cannot survive.

CORMIER, ROBERT. *The Chocolate War.*

Jerry Renault is a loner at the all-boys high school he attends. His widowed father works long hours, so Jerry is alone at home too. His introspection about the boredom and routine of life is manifested in a poster hanging in his locker, which asks "Do I Dare Disturb the Universe?" The opportunity to take this risk arises when the gang that runs the school, the Vigils, decides that Jerry should refuse to sell chocolates during the annual sale to raise money for the school. At first Jerry enjoys the attention that his refusal commands from the student body, but then the Vigils decide Jerry should sell chocolates. At this point, Jerry deliberates long and hard about whether it's time "to disturb the universe." His choice not to follow the Vigils' orders leads to a tragic circumstance for Jerry.

Theme Connector

Jerry Renault and Hamlet exist in diseased worlds. When Hamlet returns to court, after his father's death, his uncle has proclaimed himself King of Denmark and married Hamlet's mother. Hamlet is disturbed about the marriage and about the lack of a respectful period of mourning for his father, the former King of Denmark. Jerry attends a parochial high school whose headmaster, Brother Leon, relies on a gang, the Vigils, to keep order and knowingly allows them to give students "assignments." Thus, Denmark and the high school are tainted environments. Because Hamlet and Jerry have consciences that will not allow them to tolerate injustices, they must decide on a dangerous course of action. Hamlet's choice "To be or not to be . . ." and Jerry's choice "Do I dare disturb the universe?" exemplify their willingness to confront evil alone, without moral support from any adult. Neither Hamlet nor Jerry is able to survive in a diseased world.

Other YAL titles that reflect some of these same themes are:

Brooks, Bruce. *The Moves Make the Man.** Jerome tells the story of his friend Bix, who refuses to make the "moves" in dealing with his stepfather.

Brooks, Martha. *Two Moons in August.* Sidonie's family refuses to deal with her mother's death.

Childress, Alice. *Rainbow Jordan.** Rainbow faces urban life and temptation without much support from her traveling mother.

Cole, Brock. *Celine*. Artistic Celine has to find herself without parental guidance.

Cormier, Robert. *I Am the Cheese*. Adam Farmer is searching for truth in a corrupt society.

Crutcher, Chris. *Staying Fat for Sarah Byrnes*. Eric Calhoun proves that adolescent jocks can be compassionate.

———. *The Crazy Horse Electric Game*.* Willie has to leave home when his physical handicap makes him unacceptable to peers and parents.

Fox, Paula. *Monkey Island*.* Clay is homeless in New York City after his father and mother abandon him.

———————————— / / / ————————————

Julius Caesar by William Shakespeare

Themes

1. betrayal
2. tyranny of the group
3. sacrificing ethics for the group
4. leaders who abuse power

Suggested YAL titles that share some of these key themes:

MYERS, WALTER DEAN. *Scorpions*.*

Jamal, who is 12 years old, lives in Harlem with his mother and younger sister. His older brother, Randy, is in prison for holding up and killing a deli owner. Randy used to be the gang leader of the Scorpions; his "war lord," Mach, names Jamal the new leader of the Scorpions and persuades him to carry a gun. Jamal is confused about the Scorpions and doesn't share his concern with his mother, but he confides in his best friend, Tito, who tries to convince Jamal not to carry the gun. Because Tito cares about Jamal he accompanies him to a secret meeting with other Scorpions members, who confront Jamal about leadership. The meeting ends in tragedy; Jamal loses his best friend and faces survival in Harlem alone.

Theme Connector

Jamal is artistic and not interested in joining his brother's gang, the Scorpions. He allows himself to be manipulated into a dangerous situation because he cannot bring himself to say no to the gang. Jamal's gang and Brutus's group of conspirators share a common goal—to usurp power, to use power for personal gain. Brutus is manipulated by the conspirators into believing that Julius Caesar is evil and is going to destroy the republic. Therefore, Brutus joins the conspiracy "for the good of Rome." Jamal is a victim of the group; the tyranny of the group pervades his survival. Brutus becomes the leader of the group, but his conspiracy fails because he trusts deceitful men. Both Jamal and Brutus fail because they are unable to perceive the truth about the motives of the gang and the conspirators.

CORMIER, ROBERT. *We All Fall Down.*

After Buddy joins his buddies in trashing the Jeromes' house and assaulting their 14-year-old daughter, his conscience begins to gnaw at him. His three friends interpret their act as a symbol of unity and loyalty to one another, but Buddy can't laugh or joke about it. He "arranges" to meet 16-year-old Jane Jerome and becomes friendly with her. Not only does he learn about the effect this act of vandalism and assault has had on the Jerome family, but he begins to confide in Jane about his own family problems. He is repentant over his participation in the act of violence, but Jane ends their friendship when she finds out that he was part of the gang. Buddy finds out too late that he made a rotten decision when he went along with the group. The loss of Jane's friendship is irreplaceable.

Theme Connector

Brutus wrestles with his decision before joining the conspiracy to assassinate Julius Caesar. However, after Caesar's death he begins to question the conspirators' motives in killing Caesar. Perhaps he realizes he joined the conspiracy too quickly. Buddy doesn't question his friends' decision to trash the Jeromes' house—spreading excrement on the walls, tearing apart furniture, breaking windows, and worst of all, assaulting the 14-year-old daughter so badly that she falls into a coma. He doesn't feel remorse until he listens to, observes, and questions his friends, who feel no regrets. But Buddy cannot ignore his conscience; and after developing a friendship with Jane Jerome, his guilt becomes intolerable. Brutus and Buddy participate in evil deeds without any real reason. Brutus cannot accuse Julius Caesar of abusing the rights of Roman citizens; Buddy cannot give any reason for his participation in vandalizing the Jerome house. Both Brutus and Buddy realize too late that their decisions were destructive acts that might have been unnecessary, and that they destroyed their relationships with people who were important to them.

The tyranny of the group and the ability of the group to manipulate individual minds and ideals are powerful themes in both *Julius Caesar* and *We All Fall Down*. Both Buddy and Brutus do not recognize "group mentality"; they do not understand that "the group" is not necessarily interested in justice or equality or ethics.

Other YAL titles that tie into some of these themes are:

Cormier, Robert. *The Chocolate War*. Jerry Renault decides to "disturb the universe" and refuses to sell chocolates during the school's annual sale. He puts himself in jeopardy with the Vigils and Brother Leon.

Crutcher, Chris. *Running Loose*.* Louie Banks stands up to the football coach and the principal when he makes a moral choice.

Dickinson, Peter. *Eva*. Eva defies the scientific establishment and leads a group of chimps to safety.

Duncan, Lois. *Killing Mr. Griffin*. Sue McConnell finds out that the popular group accepts her when they need to use her as a decoy.

Hobbs, Will. *Downriver*.* Jessie finds out that Troy is no leader when he is willing to risk the group's lives.

Mazer, Norma Fox. *Out of Control*. After three high school friends sexually harass a girl in the hallway, one of them begins to realize how wrong his action was.

————————————————————— / / / —————————————————————

Lord of the Flies by William Golding

Themes

1. loss of innocence
2. good versus evil
3. the abuse of power by the group
4. the tyranny of the group
5. taking a stand for one's personal beliefs
6. the need for rules to foster civilized behavior

Suggested YAL titles that share some of these key themes:

HOBBS, WILL. *Downriver*.*

The setting is the Grand Canyon, where a group of misfits are enrolled in an outdoor program, "Discovery Unlimited." When their counselor, Al, leaves them in the van on their way to a rafting journey, they steal the van, unload the rafting equipment, and decide to go "downriver" on their own. Although they have spent weeks training for this adventure, the dynamics of the group, the splintered leadership, and the lack of shared decision-making turn this journey into a life-threatening experience. Their foolhardy decision to go alone, to ridicule Al's training and preparation, and to ignore survival rules nearly results in a tragedy. After their experience, they begin to realize the need for order, respect, and shared decision-making. Jessie, the narrator, shares her objective point of view about the members of the group and their roles in this daring adventure.

Theme Connector

Downriver shows what happens when a leader abuses his power. When Troy suggests that the group steal Al's van, he becomes the leader of the rafting expedition by default. Troy shares similar character traits with Jack, the leader of the hunters in *Lord of the Flies*. Like Jack, Troy manipulates the group, daring them to ignore authority and rules. However, unlike the hunters, the group in *Downriver* begins to recognize the weaknesses of Troy's leadership, especially when he puts their lives in jeopardy. Troy and Jack use similar language to cajole their peers into disregarding rules and rational behaviors.

DUNCAN, LOIS. *Killing Mr. Griffin.*

Sue McConnell is a "grind." When a group of "popular" kids lure her into participating in a prank against their English teacher, Mr. Griffin, she does not question their motives. She is flattered to be included and does not question the plan. When the prank results in Mr. Griffin's death and the police question her, Sue begins to realize that the group leader, Mark, has manipulated them for his own purpose. When she begins to see through Mark's deceit and manipulation, he tries to threaten her. But Sue, no longer able to tolerate his evil behavior, follows her conscience.

Theme Connector

Because Mark failed English, he seeks revenge against Mr. Griffin, the English teacher. He convinces a group of friends that his planned prank against Mr. Griffin is harmless. His deceit and manipulation cause the death of the teacher and place the group of friends in jeopardy with the police. Mark's evil motives parallel Jack's manipulation of the younger boys in *Lord of the Flies*. Sue McConnell's character is identified more with Ralph and Piggy; she is altruistic and is aware of right and wrong. Finally, she realizes that she has to stand up to Mark's evil nature. Both she and Ralph survive life-threatening situations.

GREENE, BETTE. *The Drowning of Stephan Jones.*

Carla is a freshman in high school who is infatuated with Andy Harris, the son of a hardware store owner. In the opening chapter of the novel, Carla witnesses Andy's father lashing out at a homosexual couple. Carla's mother, the local librarian, has encouraged Carla to be an independent and liberal-minded thinker; however, Carla's blind infatuation with Andy prevents her from recognizing Andy's combination of religious zeal and prejudice against gay people. She wants to believe Andy when he talks about his religious beliefs, but his threatening phone calls to Stephan Jones and Frank Montgomery haunt her conscience. Andy's delight in his homophobia becomes unbearable to Carla, in particular on prom night when Andy and his friends harass Stephan Jones on a bridge and throw him into the river, where he drowns. The small-town Arkansas community refuses to convict Andy and his friends of murder, despite Carla's testimony. Carla is completely disillusioned about the justice system and religious zealots.

Theme Connector

Both Ralph and Carla are idealists who believe in the basic decency of each individual. Ralph ignores Jack's zeal in organizing the hunters, and in encouraging them to paint their bodies like savages and dress "native." Ralph wants to organize the boys so that they will be rescued; he tries to instill order by building a shelter, finding food, and establishing an area for toilets. When he is hunted and threatened by Jack and his followers, Ralph recognizes Jack's evil nature. Carla allows her romantic interest in Andy to cloud her honest perception of his evil behavior. When he spews out his religious zeal and calls Frank and Stephan "faggots," she remains silent instead of questioning Andy's intolerance. Her silence tortures her, and eventually she too must confront her own sense of morality after Andy and his friends cause the death of Stephan Jones. The community protects Andy, and justice is not served from Carla's point of view. Unlike Ralph, there is no rescue for Carla; she becomes alienated from her community. She and Ralph are strong examples of idealistic adolescents trying to maintain a sense of order in their communities.

Other YAL titles that reflect some of these same themes are:

Avi. *The True Confessions of Charlotte Doyle*.* Charlotte Doyle witnesses evil during her voyage on the *Seahawk* with the cruel Captain Jaggery.

Cormier, Robert. *The Chocolate War*. Jerry Renault finds that taking a stand for what he believes in leads to alienation and violence.

Crutcher, Chris. *Running Loose*.* Louie Banks learns about corruption and evil from his coach, who is willing to win at any cost.

Davis, Terry. *If Rock and Roll Were a Machine*. Bert Bowden learns to cope with the vagaries of the adult world with the help of a vintage Harley-Davidson and some supportive adults.

Mazer, Norma Fox. *Out of Control*. When Rollo and his buddies sexually harass Valerie, he has second thoughts and wants to talk to Valerie about the situation.

Strasser, Todd. *The Wave*. A group of students in California study the forces that control a mass movement; however, the situation turns into a negative experience.

—————————————————— / / / ——————————————————

The Odyssey by Homer

Themes

1. the journey, search, or quest to prove oneself
2. the hero returning from a challenge or test
3. the courage to face one's destiny

Suggested YAL titles that share some of these key themes:

PAULSEN, GARY. *Woodsong.*
Gary Paulsen describes his profound experiences with his sled dogs in northern Minnesota, experiences that lead to his journey—completing the Iditarod. After some friends give him four sled dogs, he learns to understand these dogs—about running and feeding them, breeding and raising them, and coming to know the "dance of the dogs." As he learns their "dance," he begins to understand the innate intelligence of the dogs. In describing his journeys with the dogs, he illustrates that they have what we consider human qualities such as courage, teamwork, perseverance, loyalty, trust, and compassion. As Paulsen lives and works with the dogs Cookie, Wilson, Columbia, Storm, Yogi, and Olaf, the dogs change him; he decides to no longer hunt and kill for sport. As he observes their behaviors more and more, he begins to realize that the dogs—and therefore probably all animals—may be as complex as human beings. But because he has established a rapport with the dogs, he cannot stop running with them. He decides to run the Iditarod, the Alaskan sled dog race from Anchorage to Nome (1,100 plus miles!). During the Iditarod he gains knowledge from the dogs about himself in relation to nature, animals, and other wonders of the universe. This autobiographical experience is poetic and insightful.

Theme Connector

The Odyssey is the story of Odysseus's ten-year journey from Troy to Ithaka after the Trojan War. Because Odysseus has incurred the wrath of the god Poseidon after blinding Poseidon's son, Odysseus and his army are constantly delayed and blown off course by Poseidon. They have to combat such challenges as monsters, the Lotus Eaters, seductive women (e.g., Kalypso, the Sirens, and Kirke), Apollo's sacred cattle, whirlpools, thunderbolts, gale winds, and Zeus himself. In contrast, Paulsen is challenged by the forces of nature and his own supernatural force—his mind—but by choice. When Odysseus relates his journey to the Skherians, he explains the life-threatening forces that challenged him and his army at every port; but he does not reveal his own weakness for beautiful women and his determination to experience everything (e.g., he put wax in his sailors' ears and had the men lash him to the mast of the boat so he could be the first man to hear and to escape from the songs of the Sirens). Odysseus is unable to repress his hubris because he cannot resist any challenge.

Paulsen's challenge is different—he and his team are almost one force running in harmony, trying to coexist with nature. Unlike Odysseus, they do not have to contend with the gods. But like Odysseus, they meet up with life-threatening challenges—both internal and external: experiencing hallucinations caused by sleep deprivation; losing the trail; keeping the dogs fed so they remain healthy; dealing with frostbite, whiteouts, and severe below-zero temperatures.

There are situations and experiences in both journeys that are comparable: the song of the Sirens and the songs of the dogs; the fear of the Kyklopes and Polyphemos by Odysseus and his men, and Paulsen's fear of crossing the Alaskan mountains; Odysseus hanging on to a tree while his boat and crew go through Skylla and Kharybdis, Paulsen tied to the sled, unable to steer or stop the dogs. While Paulsen is respectful and compassionate of his dogs, Odysseus is willing to risk the lives of his men to satisfy his curiosity.

There are many other similarities between *Woodsong* and *The Odyssey*. Both journeys require similar tests or challenges. Both journeys reflect courage, tenacity, and resilience—qualities we admire in heroes. Homer's epic poem and Paulsen's autobiographical essay are strong examples of the endurance of the human spirit. The metaphorical journey, the characterizations, the poetic view of nature, and the individual's place in the universe provide a thoughtful reading experience for students.

EHRLICH, AMY. *Where It Stops, Nobody Knows*.

Nina and her mother, Joyce, decide to unload their van and live in Montpelier, Vermont. It seems like a nice community and, as Nina, the narrator, mentions, "nobody asked Joyce any questions." Nina has moved 14 times in the past 13 years, so she easily acclimates to Montpelier. But this time is different because she becomes rooted in the community—she becomes a star basketball player and begins to make lots of new friends. Then Joyce decides they must leave. As Nina grows away from her very close relationship with Joyce, tensions build. Their relationship is tested as they start a journey from Utah to Venice, California, and finally end up in Brooklyn, New York. When Nina looks back on her journey, she fondly recalls the good and bad times she's had with Joyce.

Theme Connector

Nina's journey involves real-life situations that challenge her as a developing adolescent. Nina exhibits many of the character traits of Odysseus: she is brave, confrontational, defiant, and curious; yet she is loyal to Joyce. Because Joyce is evasive and secretive, Nina finds it difficult to continue to accept Joyce's decisions. Nina continues on the journey with Joyce, despite evidence she has collected about Joyce's dubious family background. In a sense Nina is as fearless as Odysseus, when she is in dangerous situations: the Venice police looking for Joyce; Joyce abandoning the van, changing their names, and dyeing their hair; and Joyce hiding in the Brooklyn apartment. Nina is almost fearless in her attempt to be loyal to Joyce. She meets different characters along the way who help her (e.g., Sam in Montpelier); she also takes risks in certain dangerous situations (e.g., her secret friendship with hippies in Logan, Utah). By the end of the novel the FBI arrives at their Brooklyn apartment to arrest Joyce, and Nina learns the truth about her mother. Nina is a well-developed character; her journey—like Odysseus's— shows how she uses her wits and endurance to survive challenging circumstances.

Other YAL novels that tie into these themes are:

Bridgers, Sue Ellen. *Permanent Connections*. Rural North Carolina provides Rob with the strength to face his worst enemy—himself.

Brooks, Bruce. *Midnight Hour Encores*. Sixteen-year-old Sibilance Spooner journeys cross-country with her father and her cello to discover herself.

Buss, Frank Leeper. *Journey of the Sparrows*.* Maria, a 14-year-old El Salvadoran, describes her family's journey through Mexico to Chicago as illegal aliens.

Carter, Alden R. *Up Country*. Carl is a loner until he travels "up country" and finds himself.

Cole, Brock. *The Goats*.* Howie and Laurie face many obstacles on their journey and prove they can meet any challenge.

Hobbs, Will. *Downriver*.* A group of misfits prove they can survive the Colorado River without their guide.

Paulsen, Gary. *The River*. Brian Robeson returns to the Canadian wilderness and manages to float a raft down the river to save a man's life.

_____ . *The Voyage of the Frog*. David Alspeth takes the journey of his life and manages to survive sharks and tankers in his tiny sailboat.

Rylant, Cynthia. *Missing May*. When May dies, Summer and Ob search for a medium to help them find May's spirit.

———————————————— / / / ————————————————

Of Mice and Men by John Steinbeck

Themes

1. exclusion from mainstream society
2. surviving poverty, prejudice, and brutality
3. holding on to friends who are loyal
4. the dignity of each individual

Suggested YAL titles that share some of these key themes:

FOX, PAULA. *Monkey Island.**

Twelve-year-old Clay Garrity suddenly finds himself homeless and parentless in New York City. After Clay's father loses his job and can't find employment, he abandons Clay and his pregnant wife. They lose their apartment and have to live in a "welfare hotel." When Clay comes home from school one day, he finds some money and stale doughnuts and a note from his mother, who cannot cope with their horrific living conditions. Clay decides to leave after the woman next door mentions the welfare department. He grabs a few belongings and leaves the hotel, wandering around the streets of New York. Eventually he finds two men, Buddy and Calvin, who live in a small park. They share their food and cardboard shelter with Clay. Every day Clay watches the hotel in case his mother returns, but she doesn't, so he goes back to Buddy and Calvin. When Clay catches pneumonia, Buddy takes him to the hospital. Social services then place Clay in a caring foster home and help him find his mother. The main part of the story involves the friendship and protection that Buddy and Calvin offer Clay. This novel illustrates the problems that confront the homeless as they struggle to survive in New York City. Clay's friendship with Buddy and Calvin provide him with a feeling of security. After being reunited with his mother, Clay finds Buddy to thank him for his help.

Theme Connector

Like the characters Lennie and George in *Of Mice and Men*, the characters in *Monkey Island* are unconnected to mainstream society, which is indifferent to their situation. George and Lennie lead a rootless existence, always hoping to save their money to have their own place, a garden, and chickens. Lennie never gives up hope, but George sometimes recites their dream with a feeling of doubt. Clay is confused about reconnecting to family life—he understands how painful family life can be; what he experiences is hopelessness and despair. Characters in both novels "slip through the cracks" of society: George and Lennie are on the run because of Lennie's inability to act sensibly in social situations; Clay runs away from the welfare hotel, and neither the school system nor the welfare office catches up with him for a while. Meanwhile he finds support and friendship with Buddy and Calvin. Their support sustains Clay through his despair. George and Lennie's friendship and loyalty sustain them as they move from place to place, until the incident with Curley's wife. George protects Lennie and treats him with dignity, although he sometimes feels very little hope for their future. But it is Lennie's undivided loyalty and friendship that keep George going, just as Buddy's caring for Clay connects these characters. Buddy, a homeless black man from the South, shows great compassion for Clay, comparable to George's loyalty to Lennie.

Both plots reveal societies that treat these characters as "throwaway people." *Monkey Island* has a positive ending: Clay is reunited with his mother. But Clay never forgets Buddy's friendship and support. Both novels sensitize readers to the continuing poverty and neglect in American society. Both novels present a positive view of characters who are loyal, caring, and trusting, trying to find their place in society.

GIBBONS, KAYE. *Ellen Foster.* *

The narrator of this novel is a young southern girl who is abandoned by a vicious father after her mother dies. She "makes her way," staying with some "Negroes" down the road, too proud to eat their food because she is white. After finding the situation intolerable, she goes to live with her well-to-do grandmother, who abhors her. Because the narrator's mother married beneath her social class, the grandmother considers her grandaughter "poor white trash." She treats her like a Negro, sending her into the fields to pick cotton. When the grandmother dies, the girl is placed in a foster home where she finds love and support for the first time in her life. She changes her name to Ellen Foster. Told in flashback by an adult recalling her deprived childhood, this is a richly textured story about an abandoned child who manages to survive.

Theme Connector

Ellen Foster and *Of Mice and Men* share a view of characters stuck in poverty, existing day-by-day. Both novels illustrate the effects of poverty on people searching for their place in society. The dialogue by the ranch owner in *Of Mice and Men* and the one by the father and grandmother in *Ellen Foster* clearly convey contempt towards these rootless characters. The "castoffs" manage to maintain their sense of dignity because they find friendship and trust—George and Lennie have each other; Ellen finds protection with a black family and a foster family. Both novels express the dignity of these characters and their ability to survive in an uncaring society.

Some other YAL titles that tie into these themes are:

Bridgers, Sue Ellen. *Home before Dark*. After living as migrant workers for many years, Stella Mae's family settles down on her uncle's farm.

Childress, Alice. *Rainbow Jordan*.* Rainbow learns to survive in the city without much support from adults.

Cole, Brock. *The Goats*.* Howie and Laura develop a strong friendship after they are abandoned on Goat Island.

Cormier, Robert. *The Bumblebee Flies Anyway*. Barney and his friends, who are patients in a hospital cancer ward, organize a quest to reach a goal.

Covington, Dennis. *Lizard*.* Lucius Sims, called "Lizard" because of his deformed face, goes on a journey and gains respect.

Crutcher, Chris. *The Crazy Horse Electric Game*.* Willie learns to survive with a handicap after being the athletic hero in his school.

———. *Staying Fat for Sarah Byrnes*. Eric proves the true meaning of friendship when he sticks by Sarah Byrnes.

Davis, Terry. *If Rock and Roll Were a Machine*. An experience with a teacher in fourth grade changes the course of Bert Bowden's life until he gets his Harley-Davidson.

Doherty, Berlie. *Dear Nobody*. Helen and Chris deal with teenage pregnancy and loss of love and friendship.

Hesse, Karen. *Phoenix Rising*. After a nuclear radiation leak, Nyle and her grandmother show compassion for Ezra and his mother, who are outcasts in their community.

Hinton, S. E. *The Outsiders*. Ponyboy explains what it feels like to be outside the mainstream.

Sebestyen, Ouida. *Words by Heart*.* Lena's father makes her realize the dignity of every human life despite the prejudice they experience.

Thesman, Jean. *Where the Road Ends*. Mary Jack, a foster child, yearns for a family. When a situation presents itself, she rises to the challenge.

——————————————— / / / ———————————————

Romeo and Juliet by William Shakespeare

Themes

1. innocent love and friendship
2. dealing with death; dealing with suicide
3. family isolation

Suggested YAL titles that share some of these key themes:

GREENE, BETTE. *Summer of My German Soldier*.

Patty Bergen, a 12-year-old Jewish girl living in Arkansas during World War II, helps an escaped German prisoner of war, Anton. Patty has a distant relationship with her mother, father, and peers. She lives on the edge of her community; and when the opportunity to help Anton arises, she makes a commitment without considering the consequences. Eventually Anton is shot while trying to escape, and Patty is tried for treason.

Theme Connector

Young people like Patty and Romeo and Juliet are innocents who listen to their hearts. Romeo and Juliet are victims of a family feud that has no meaning to them; Patty has no positive relationship with her father and mother, so she builds a relationship with a German prisoner of war. Patty's relationship could not be more humiliating to her Jewish parents, but Patty reacts to Anton's need on a humane level. Her relationship is doomed, as is Romeo and Juliet's. Because of their youthful innocence, neither Patty nor Romeo and Juliet understand yet the control adults have over their lives. They proceed to make decisions on the basis of their own needs, without considering any repercussions. Romeo and Juliet are naive enough to think they can escape the hostile adult world, but their plan for escape results in their deaths. Patty follows her heart because she finds little if any understanding from society. In some ways, the character of Patty is more tragic because she expects the worst from society.

PECK, RICHARD. *Remembering the Good Times*.

The narrator, Buck Mendenhall, shares all the "good times" he and Kate and Travis had in high school. Their trust of and loyalty to one another is poignant, because they are each so different. Buck is witty and happy-go-lucky, Kate is wise and thoughtful, and Travis is a brilliant student. They hang around at the home of Kate's grandmother, playing cards and discussing their plans to be together. However, Buck and Kate are not aware of Travis's relationship with his parents. Travis's subsequent suicide is devastating to Buck and Kate. Buck tries to recount the details and events that preceded the suicide; he looks for signals that he and Katie might have ignored. They mourn Travis, trying to understand. At a special meeting with members of the community, Travis's parents speak; but it is Katie's grandmother who reminds the community that it is everyone's responsibility to care about one another.

Theme Connector

As in *Romeo and Juliet*, the Kirbys assume that their son Travis is a "good, well-adjusted boy." He is a brilliant student who has friends; and his upper-class parents, like the upper-class Capulets and Montagues, presume that he will continue to demonstrate socially acceptable behavior. Although Romeo and Juliet do not plan to commit suicide, they use Juliet's "disguised death" as a solution to their problem. With the help of her nurse and Friar Laurence, Juliet takes a potion so that her family thinks she is dead. Then when Romeo returns, he will meet her in the tomb, she will wake up, and they will leave Verona. Travis, who is as isolated from his parents as Romeo and Juliet are from theirs, does not have adults as confidants. He is isolated—almost estranged—from his parents and commits suicide to solve his dilemma. Juliet, in her innocence, weaves a plan involving a make-believe death, never considering death as a reality; Travis too weaves his plan around death, but his death is a reality.

DAVIS, JENNY. *Sex Education.*

Sixteen-year-old Livvie Sinclair and David Kindler become best friends as partners in a biology project. Livvie and David exhibit their kindness and thoughtfulness for Maggie, their "Caring Project." As they learn about the dangers in Maggie's relationship with her husband, they begin making decisions without consulting any adults—neither their parents nor their biology teacher. Because their own relationship is so strong and they are falling in love, they naively believe they can handle Maggie's problems alone. But they cannot, and after David accidentally dies, Livvie blames herself. At a psychiatric institution she starts writing her journal, which describes her experiences with David learning about caring, loving, and pain.

Theme Connector

The quality of innocent love and friendship is a common theme in both the novel and *Romeo and Juliet.* Scenes from the play that depict Romeo and Juliet's developing relationship could be compared with the dialogue between Livvie and David as they develop their friendship and as they become sexually attracted to each other. Also, Romeo and Juliet plan secretly, as do Livvie and David, neither couple confiding in parents. The novel and the play show how adolescents build a relationship on qualities such as trust, loyalty, and consideration, along with physical attraction. *Sex Education* is sensitively written; David and Livvie are well-developed characters who are believable. Unlike Romeo and Juliet, they do not enlist the assistance of a nurse or a Friar Laurence. Their biology teacher realizes too late that Livvie and David assumed too much responsibility in their "Caring Project."

Other YAL titles that share some of these same themes are:

Arrick, Fran. *Tunnel Vision.* A blunt and honest narrative about Anthony's suicide, from multiple perspectives.

Blume, Judy. *Tiger Eyes*. Davey has to face truths inside herself after her father is killed.

Carter, Alden R. *Sheila's Dying*. Jerry Kincaid finds inner strength when he helps a very ill Sheila.

Crutcher, Chris. *Chinese Handcuffs*. Dillon probes deep inside himself to understand and to overcome overwhelming circumstances.

Naughton, Jim. *My Brother Stealing Second*. After his brother's death, Bobby is waiting for his family to become whole again.

Zindel, Paul. *The Pigman*. John and Lorraine want to proclaim their innocence in Mr. Pignati's death.

—————————— / / / ——————————

The Scarlet Letter by Nathaniel Hawthorne

Themes

1. women's place in Puritan times
2. alienation of the individual from his/her community
3. Puritan obsession with fear, guilt, sin
4. Puritan repression of sexuality
5. the individual's courage to survive injustice

Suggested YAL titles that share some of these key themes:

AVI. *Nothing but the Truth*.

Philip Malloy has a D in English; thus, he is ineligible for the track team. He claims that his English teacher, Miss Narwin, doesn't like him. When she disciplines him for humming the National Anthem out loud during home room when he's supposed to be silent, he is suspended by the vice-principal. Philip never admits that he has broken school rules by humming the anthem; he convinces his parents and a candidate for the Board of Education that the teacher is not allowing him to be patriotic. The media escalate this situation, until his dedicated teacher and Philip are both alienated from the school community.

Theme Connector

This YA novel presents the reader with a series of events that illustrate the alienation of individuals from their community. In his quest to be eligible for track at all costs, Philip allows public opinion to condemn his English teacher. The newspaper, radio stations, and the public decide that Philip was being patriotic; Philip never publicly disagrees with this perception. Philip's passive behavior could be compared to Arthur Dimmesdale's position in the Puritan community. Revered and adored as a pillar of the community, Dimmesdale suffers from his "patriotism" too. Unable to confess publicly to his act of adultery, he allows the public to scorn Hester Prynne.

Like *The Scarlet Letter*, the YA novel *Nothing But the Truth* illustrates the group's willingness to revile and to isolate the individual from his/her community. However, Philip is a teenager who does not possess the courage, the wisdom, or the tenacity of Hester Prynne. After Miss Narwin leaves, Philip is unable to survive the contempt of his peer group; he enrolls in a private school. Hester, however, remains on the outskirts of her community and transcends the Puritans' hypocrisy.

ZINDEL, PAUL. *The Pigman.*

Trying to assuage their guilt, two adolescents, John and Lorraine, explain the death of Mr. Pignati, an older Italian man who befriended and trusted them. Were they responsible for his death? Writing a chapter-by-chapter account of their relationship with Mr. Pignati, John feels that they did not cause Mr. Pignati's death, while Lorraine disagrees with John. She feels that they treated Mr. Pignati's friendship lightly. In retelling the events that led to Mr. Pignati's death, John and Lorraine are transformed; they will never be the same again. Mr. Pignati proved to them that they are adults who can be loved and trusted; he touched their consciousness. They cannot "hide out" from the adult world; they have to become responsible for their actions as members of society.

Theme Connector

In contrast to Hester Prynne, John and Lorraine do not accept the rules of society, whether in their school community or at home. They ridicule the adult world, including parents. Because Mr. Pignati is an adult, they are careless with his trust, respect, and love for them. They learn after his death that human relationships are serious and cannot be dismissed frivolously. Hester, although treated with disdain by the Puritan community, is unfailingly dignified. Condemned to wear the Scarlet Letter A for Adulteress, she sets an example as a productive member of the Puritan community—she sews shrouds for corpses; she designs elegant stitchery for members of the clergy; she is a good parent; she is a model of integrity. John and Lorraine write their story to sort out their feelings of guilt. They begin to wonder if their self-imposed isolation from the rules of society makes them responsible for Mr. Pignati's death. Their telephone games are over; their escapades in the zoo and their beer drinking in the cemetery are no longer funny. Their regret over Mr. Pignati's death cannot assuage their guilt; however, like Hester, they will learn to live with their guilt.

STAPLES, SUZANNE FISHER. *Shabanu.**

Shabanu, a Pakistani adolescent who adores her parents, is in conflict with her culture's system of arranging marriage. When she is betrothed to a 52-year old magistrate, she is torn between her independent spirit and her culture's expectations for women. In discussing traditions and choices with her independent aunt, she realizes that she cannot bear to leave her family. Shabanu's sense of responsibility prevails eventually, and she returns to her family, realizing that no one can penetrate or destroy her inner spirit. Shabanu shares Hester's indomitable inner strength, determined spirit, and canny wisdom. Her outward behavior becomes as dignified as Hester's, once she accepts her destiny.

Theme Connector

Two women, Hester Prynne and Shabanu, have to survive in seemingly impossible circumstances; but through personal introspection and innate intelligence, they confront their destiny. The comparison and contrast of harshness and domination of the Puritan and Pakistani cultures illuminate the courage and strength of both female protagonists. Shabanu is a thoroughly developed character who shares many of Hester's traits, especially a sense of self-worth and dignity. They are strong examples of gender oppression in two distinct cultures.

CARY, LORENE. *Black Ice.**

A young urban African-American teenager, Lorene Carey, becomes a scholarship student at a prestigious prep school in New Hampshire. In an honest voice, she describes her experiences at St. Paul's, especially her feelings of inferiority as one of the few token blacks, her anger at preppy traditions, and her own insecurity. When she returns many years later as an English teacher and member of the Board of Trustees, she realizes that she was responsible for her own feelings of isolation and alienation from her peers. She realizes that she missed an opportunity to teach her peers about her "black experience." This autobiography is a thoughtful analysis of being an outsider—a feeling shared by many adolescents.

Theme Connector

In contrast to Hester, Lorene as a teenager is feisty and confronts her white peers constantly. As an adult looking back and writing about her experiences at St. Paul's, she, like Hester, gains wisdom and objectivity. She realizes that she, too, imparted some knowledge to St. Paul's students: "they were up against those of us who'd lived a real life in the real world." Lorene Carey confronts racism whereas Hester Prynne confronts hypocrisy—both women demonstrate courage and intelligence.

Other excellent books for young adults provide additional historical background about the Puritans. These include:

Clapp, Patricia. *Witches' Children: A Story of Salem.* Mary Warren tells about her involvement in accusing Salem villagers of witchcraft and how her guilt haunts her.

Petry, Ann. *Tituba of Salem Village.** In 1692 in Salem Village, the minister's slave, Tituba, can predict the future. This story is based on a historical account.

Rinaldi, Ann. *A Break with Charity.* This story about the Salem witch trials provides thorough information about the accusers and the accused.

Speare, Elizabeth George. *The Witch of Blackbird Pond.* After her parents die, Kit, a teenager, is sent to New England to live with her aunt and uncle. She finds her uncle's Puritanical ways to be harsh and limiting. She meets an older woman, a Quaker, who is comforting and friendly. But because the woman will not bend to the Puritan code, the community considers her a witch. Kit defends her and nurses her when she is ill, thereby alienating herself from her relatives. Kit herself is tried as a witch and is forced to leave the Puritan community.

Many YA novels share broader themes with *The Scarlet Letter*, such as searching for self (change and growth), coming-of-age, choosing to reject the hypocrisy of one's community, facing a moral choice, being alienated from peers, and surviving under extreme circumstances (acting with grace under fire). Some YAL titles that reflect these thematic ideas are:

Bridgers, Sue Ellen. *Permanent Connections.* When Rob has to stay with family in rural North Carolina, he learns about helping others.

Carter, Alden R. *Sheila's Dying.* Jerry shows his compassion and loyalty when he learns that Sheila is dying.

Crutcher, Chris. *The Crazy Horse Electric Game.** When his peers and parents become squeamish about Willie's disability, he leaves his community.

Davis, Terry. *If Rock and Roll Were a Machine.* Bert Bowden recalls an injustice in school that alienated him from his friends and his parents.

Hinton, S. E. *The Outsiders.* Sodapop, Ponyboy, and Darry prove they can survive as "outsiders" in their community.

Lipsyte, Robert. *The Brave.** Sonny Bear leaves the Indian reservation to prove himself in New York City.

Voigt, Cynthia. *The Runner.** Bullet Tillerman is alienated from parents and peers; he joins the army to escape his community.

———————————————————— / / / ————————————————————

*To Kill a Mockingbird** by Harper Lee

Themes

1. coming-of-age; fitting into one's community
2. confronting racism, prejudice, intolerance
3. family values: compassion, tolerance
4. the innocence of children regarding prejudice

Suggested YAL titles that share some of these themes:

SEBESTYEN, OUIDA. *Words by Heart.**

Lena, a young black girl growing up in a white community, is unaware of being treated differently until she wins a Bible quotation contest. She is scorned by peers and adults in the community and doesn't understand why. A poor white family that lives nearby has been taunting Lena's father with racist remarks and threats. When her father leaves to work on a farm job and doesn't return, she sets out to find him. When Lena finally finds her father, he is wounded and dying from a gunshot. The white neighbor is wounded too, but he can be saved. Before Lena's father dies, he makes her understand the value of every human life. Lena loves and respects her father, but she has learned that she will have to deal with racism without him.

Theme Connector

Scout, the narrator of *To Kill a Mockingbird*, and Lena, the main character in *Words by Heart*, both have strong role models in their fathers. Both fathers are determined to teach their children to respect the dignity of every person, regardless of race or ethnic background. Lena and Scout are innocents who encounter an intolerant world among peers and adults. Without their fathers, they are unprotected and must learn to adapt to the cruelties of society, despite the racist remarks and acts they observe. Both realize the legacy of tolerance and compassion their fathers have modeled for them.

SHANGE, NTOZAKE. *Betsey Brown.**

Set in St. Louis, Missouri, in 1959 during the period of school integration, this coming-of-age novel focuses on 13-year-old Betsey Brown. Betsey is a talented student, a dreamer, and conscious of her black community. Her parents are professionals: her father is a surgeon and her mother is a social worker. They live in the black community, trying to make sure that their children are aware of their cultural background.

When Betsey is bused to a white school, she encounters intolerance, becomes confused about her black identity, and runs away. When she returns, her father and mother have to be honest with her about the prejudice she faces.

Theme Connector

Betsey and Scout share several personality traits: independence, free thinking, "hiding out" from the family when they think they have been treated unfairly, and curiosity. Greer, Betsey's father, is not as major a character as Atticus, but he shows a similar love and concern for Betsey. Betsey's grandmother and brothers provide her with childhood experiences that are similar to the ones Scout describes. The attitudes of peers, neighbors, teachers, and adults in the community cause Betsey the same puzzlement and anger as described in Scout's narration. Betsey and Scout are young and impressionable; they are fearless in their determination to understand their world.

MURROW, LIZA KETCHUM. *Twelve Days in August.**

Sixteen-year-old Todd O'Connor is psyched for high school soccer. He covets the starting position at left wing, and his life is flowing smoothly in a small Vermont community, until Rita and Alex Beekman, twins from Los Angeles, move to town. Alex is a natural soccer player; Todd respects his talent and offers his friendship. However, Randy Tovich, who has been the star scorer, finds Alex's natural talent threatening to his own position and stature on the team. He ridicules Alex's grace on the playing field and accuses him of being gay. Randy tries to persuade other team members to side with him, and at a scrimmage game he tries to keep Alex from getting the ball. Todd has to make a moral choice—should he stick up for Alex? What if Alex is gay? Through his agonizing decision, Todd learns about intolerance and prejudice. This novel is especially powerful because it addresses adolescent concerns about homosexuality and sports.

Theme Connector

Scout and Todd struggle to understand cutting remarks that reflect prejudice. Scout's cousin and some of the adults in her neighborhood call Atticus a "nigger lover" when he defends Tom Robinson. Scout has learned to value the dignity of each individual, so she is confused and upset by these remarks. Todd's relationship with Alex is open and friendly; Todd does not consider Alex's sexuality as a valid reason to break off his friendship with Alex. However, Todd has to deal with remarks about Alex's sexuality by Randy and other members of the team. The soccer coach, who could stop Randy from making destructive remarks, chooses to ignore the situation. Does Todd risk alienating himself from them? Both

Scout and Todd exhibit strong characteristics; they think about situations and try to figure them out. They question and try to understand different points of view, but in the end they realize that their own sense of right and wrong has to be maintained at all costs. Todd has a close relationship with his uncle, who helps him to consider Alex's point of view. Scout has Atticus, who helps her to restrain her temper. Both characters realize they must make up their own minds about confronting intolerance.

Other YAL titles that tie into these themes are:

Bridgers, Sue Ellen. *Home before Dark*. Stella Mae and her family gain a sense of community when they settle on her uncle's farm.

Cannon, A. E. *Amazing Gracie*. Gracie becomes the caretaker of her family in a new community.

Cormier, Robert. *Tunes for Bears to Dance To*. Henry learns about anti-Semitism and has to make a moral choice.

Fleischman, Paul. *The Borning Room*. A first person narrative about the strength and endurance of family values and nature's life cycle.

Guy, Rosa. *The Friends.** Phyllisia finds out about friendship and snobbery in Harlem.

Homes, A. M. *Jack*. When Jack's father reveals his homosexuality, Jack has to learn to accept his father and continue to love him.

Krisher, Trudy. *Spite Fences.** A poor white girl's view of prejudice during the 1950s civil rights movement in the South.

Paulsen, Gary. *The Monument*. Rocky's view of her life and her town is changed by Mick, an artist who teaches her to see in a new way.

OTHER TITLES TO CONSIDER

Some other titles and authors that frequently appear in curriculum guides, but are not necessarily required, share common themes with YAL.

Anne Frank's *The Diary of a Young Girl* shares with the following titles themes of alienation and the need to belong to a community:

Crew, Linda. *Children of the River.**

Greene, Bette. *Summer of My German Soldier*.

Houston, Jeanne Wakatsuki, and James D. Houston. *Farewell to Manzanar.**

Matas, Carol. *Daniel's Story*.

Uchida, Yoshiko. *The Invisible Thread.**

Watkins, Yoko Kawashima. *So Far from the Bamboo Grove.**

The themes of alienation and teenage rebellion in *The Catcher in the Rye* by J. D. Salinger are also strong in the following titles:

Bridgers, Sue Ellen. *Permanent Connections*.

Carter, Alden. *Up Country*.

Cole, Brock. *Celine*.

Cormier, Robert. *The Chocolate War*.

———. *We All Fall Down*.

Crutcher, Chris. *Chinese Handcuffs*.

———. *Running Loose*.*

Lynch, Chris. *Iceman*.

Oneal, Zibby. *The Language of Goldfish*.

Voigt, Cynthia. *The Runner*.*

Two recent science-fiction YA novels tie in with the theme of repression in a totalitarian society as shown in Ray Bradbury's *Fahrenheit 451* and George Orwell's *Nineteen Eighty-four*. They are:

Dickinson, Peter. *Eva*.

Lowry, Lois. *The Giver*.

The respect and joy in discovering the harmony in nature are detailed in Gary Paulsen's *Hatchet*, *The River*, *Woodsong*, and *The Island*. These books complement Thoreau's *Walden* and Annie Dillard's *Pilgrim at Tinker Creek*.

The Old Man and the Sea by Ernest Hemingway can be bridged with *The Bumblebee Flies Anyway* by Robert Cormier, *Downriver** by Will Hobbs, *Shabanu** by Suzanne Fisher Staples, and *The Voyage of the Frog* by Gary Paulsen. All these books reflect the journey theme.

Although some titles have a stronger connection than others, the possibilities of grouping various works are nearly endless.

ARCHETYPES

Young Adult Literature offers teachers an effective way to introduce or reinforce the study of archetypes in literature by grouping a variety of titles around archetypal situations and characters. Before or after studying a traditional classic or contemporary novel, teachers might want to introduce the concept of archetypes in literature. Based on the Jungian theory of archetypes, we can consider an archetype as character type or action which recurs frequently in literature (and art) and which evokes profound emotional response in reader or viewer because it resonates with an image already existing in the unconscious mind. (Jung 1969, 4–7).

By reading YAL that reflects archetypal patterns similar to those in classic or contemporary literature, students can more easily begin to understand the concept of recurring archetypes. By studying, discussing, and recognizing archetypes in literature, students build the foundation for making connections among various works of literature during the course of their reading lives; many students begin to grasp and identify the archetypal images and patterns that appear in new forms. Archetypes also help students become more conscious of an author's style and to think about and recognize the way in which a particular writer develops a character or story.

For example, the situational archetype of **Birth/Death/Rebirth** often presents the main character in a conflicting situation with which he or she barely can cope. Through pain and suffering, the character's spirit survives the challenge or struggle, so that he or she is able to shed feelings of despair or hopelessness. Through a process of self-realization the character is reborn. This archetypal situation is apparent in many YA novels. For example, in *Sex Education* by Jenny Davis the main character, 16-year-old Livvie, shares her journal with the reader, explaining how she and David, her biology partner, chose her neighbor, Maggie, for their Caring Project. Livvie and David discover dangerous information about Maggie and her abusive husband, and they try to protect Maggie without adult advice or support. Their solution to Maggie's problems puts them in a vulnerable position that results in David's death. Because Livvie believes she is responsible for his death, she withdraws from her community. Through sharing her journal with the reader and a therapist, she is able to reflect on her experiences with David as a time of learning about caring, pain, sex, and love.

Other YA novels with similar situational archetypes are *Permanent Connections* by Sue Ellen Bridgers and *Memory* by Margaret Mahy. Bridgers' male protagonist, Rob, rebels against his parents' middle-class values by failing in school and using drugs and alcohol. When he and his father have to travel to rural North Carolina to help care for his uncle, aunt, and grandfather, Rob's lifestyle changes abruptly. Because his father has to return to work, Rob must remain in North Carolina to help the family. Rob is angry and belligerent; but when he tangles with the law, his uncle, aunt, and grandfather support him unconditionally. Rob's attitude and behavior show the anguish and fears that adolescents suffer. Rob finally realizes the value of family love and pride through this experience.

In *Memory*, 17-year-old Johnny Dart has managed to alienate himself from his parents because of his drunken brawls. He tortures himself trying to remember how Janine, his twin sister, died. In his search he meets up with Sophie, a bag lady suffering from Alzheimer's disease. She touches a compassionate spot in Johnny—he cleans her apartment, moves in, and becomes responsible for her, eventually calling in social services. During the process he finds out that Janine's death was an accident. Through his struggles and involvement with Sophie he develops a conscience while gaining a new perspective on the possibilities within himself.

Other Situational Archetypes

Throughout this section, remember: titles that deal with multicultural themes or issues are followed by an asterisk (*).

The Fall; Expulsion from Eden. The main character is expelled because of an unacceptable action on his or her part.

YA novels that tie into this archetypal situation:

Avi. *Nothing But the Truth.*
Covington, Dennis. *Lizard.**
Doherty, Berlie. *Dear Nobody.*
Greene, Bette. *The Drowning of Stephan Jones.*
Kerr, M. E. *Deliver Us From Evie.*
_____ . *Gentlehands.*

Suggested classic/contemporary tie-in:

Hawthorne, Nathaniel. *The Scarlet Letter.*
Miller, Arthur. *The Crucible.*
Wharton, Edith. *Ethan Frome.*

The Journey. The protagonist searches for acceptance in a community; the search for meaning in one's life.

YA novels:

Carter, Alden R. *Up Country.*
Crutcher, Chris. *The Crazy Horse Electric Game.**
Hobbs, Will. *Downriver.**
Myers, Walter Dean. *Somewhere in the Darkness.**
Paulsen, Gary. *Dogsong.**
_____ . *The Island.*

Suggested classic/contemporary tie-in:

Homer. *The Odyssey.*
Steinbeck, John. *Of Mice and Men.*
Twain, Mark. *The Adventures of Huckleberry Finn.**

The Test or Trial. Rites of passage; transition from one stage of life to another. The main character experiences growth and change; he or she experiences a transformation.

YA novels:

Avi. *The True Confessions of Charlotte Doyle.**

Bell, William. *Forbidden City.**

Bridgers, Sue Ellen. *Permanent Connections.*

Brooks, Bruce. *The Moves Make the Man.**

Carter, Alden R. *Dancing on Dark Waters.*

Cooney, Caroline B. *Driver's Ed.*

Marsden, John. *So Much to Tell You.*

Myers, Walter Dean. *Fallen Angels.**

Oneal, Zibby. *The Language of Goldfish.*

Pfeffer, Susan Beth. *The Year without Michael.*

Suggested classic/contemporary tie-in:

Crane, Stephen. *The Red Badge of Courage.*

Golding, William. *Lord of the Flies.*

Morrison, Tony. *The Bluest Eye.**

Potok, Chaim. *The Chosen.*

Remarque, Erich Maria. *All Quiet on the Western Front.*

Walker, Alice. *The Color Purple.**

Annihilation; Absurdity; Total Oblivion. In order to exist in an intolerable world, the main character accepts that life is absurd, ridiculous, and ironic.

YA novels:

Cormier, Robert. *The Chocolate War.*

Crutcher, Chris. *Chinese Handcuffs.*

Davis, Terry. *If Rock and Roll Were a Machine.*

Lowry, Lois. *The Giver.*

O'Brien, Robert C. *Z for Zachariah.*

Suggested classic/contemporary tie-in:

Beckett, Samuel. *Krapp's Last Tape.*

———— . *Waiting for Godot.*

Camus, Albert. *The Stranger.*

Chute, Nevil. *On the Beach.*

Ellison, Ralph. *The Invisible Man.**

Heller, Joseph. *Catch 22.*

Vonnegut, Kurt, Jr. *Slaughterhouse Five.*

Parental Conflicts and Relationships. The protagonist deals with parental conflict by rejecting or bonding with parents.

YA novels:

Blume, Judy. *Tiger Eyes*.
Bridgers, Sue Ellen. *Home before Dark*.
Brooks, Bruce. *Midnight Hour Encores*.
Crutcher, Chris. *Ironman*.
Myers, Walter Dean. *Somewhere in the Darkness*.*
Peck, Richard. *Unfinished Portrait of Jessica*.
Voigt, Cynthia. *The Runner*.*

Suggested classic/contemporary tie-in:

Guest, Judith. *Ordinary People*.
Miller, Arthur. *Death of a Salesman*.
Shakespeare, William. *Romeo and Juliet*.
Smiley, Jane. *A Thousand Acres*.
Tan, Amy. *The Joy Luck Club*.*
Williams, Tennessee. *The Glass Menagerie*.

The Wise Old Woman or Man. This figure protects or assists the main character in facing challenges.

YA novels:

Bridgers, Sue Ellen. *Notes for Another Life*.
Hesse, Karen. *Phoenix Rising*.
Johnson, Angela. *Toning the Sweep*.*
Lasky, Kathryn. *Memoirs of a Bookbat*.
Paterson, Katherine. *Jacob Have I Loved*.
Paulsen, Gary. *The Monument*.
Peck, Richard. *Remembering the Good Times*.

Suggested classic/contemporary tie-in:

Lee, Harper. *To Kill a Mockingbird*.*
O'Neill, Eugene. *Ah, Wilderness!*
Shakespeare, William. *Romeo and Juliet*.
Steinbeck, John. *The Grapes of Wrath*.
Wilder, Thornton. *Our Town*.

The Hero. The main character leaves his or her community to go on an adventure, performing deeds that bring honor to the community. The journey of the hero.

YA novels:

Cooney, Caroline B. *Flight #116 Is Down*.

Crutcher, Chris. *Staying Fat for Sarah Byrnes*.

Davis, Terry. *If Rock and Roll Were a Machine*.

Hobbs, Will. *Beardance.**

Klass, David. *California Blue*.

Lasky, Kathryn. *Memoirs of a Bookbat*.

Taylor, Mildred D. *Roll of Thunder, Hear My Cry.**

Wolff, Virginia Euwer. *Make Lemonade.**

Suggested classic/contemporary tie-in:

Crane, Stephen. *The Red Badge of Courage*.

Dickens, Charles. *A Tale of Two Cities*.

Gaines, Ernest J. *The Autobiography of Miss Jane Pittman.**

Gardner, John. *Grendel*.

Hurston, Zora Neale. *Their Eyes Were Watching God.**

Renault, Mary. *The King Must Die*.

Rostand, Edmond. *Cyrano de Bergerac*.

Sophocles. *Antigone*.

The Sacrificial Redeemer. The protagonist is willing to die for a belief; the main character maintains a strong sense of morality.

YA novels:

Cormier, Robert. *The Bumblebee Flies Anyway*.

———— . *The Chocolate War*.

Crutcher, Chris. *Ironman*.

Krisher, Trudy. *Spite Fences.**

Lasky, Kathryn. *Memoirs of a Bookbat*.

Myers, Walter Dean. *Scorpions.**

Paulsen, Gary. *Nightjohn.**

Suggested classic/contemporary tie-in:

Bolt, Robert. *A Man for All Seasons*.

O'Neill, Eugene. *Mourning Becomes Electra*.

Shakespeare, William. *Julius Caesar*.

Sophocles. *Antigone*.

Many additional titles can be grouped with these archetypal situations. Using YAL will reinforce students' understanding of the recurring patterns in literature and make them more meaningful.

THEMATIC EXTENSIONS

Finding the right books to pair is not easy, but the more books you read yourself, the more possibilities you'll begin to see. Furthermore, you need not stop with a single pairing. A short story, a poem, a scene from a play, or a magazine or newspaper article—better yet, several of those—can be used to introduce a unit, make comparisons, reinforce a point during the discussion, or pull loose ends together at the end of the unit.

For example, instead of "teaching" Erich Maria Remarque's *All Quiet on the Western Front* in and for itself, expand the concept so that the class examines literature about war and how people respond to it. That allows you to incorporate all kinds of literary works into the unit. Following are some of the possibilities from which to choose:

- Because contemporary teenagers are likely to be more interested in the Vietnam War than in World War I, you might want to have them first read *Fallen Angels** by Walter Dean Myers, a powerful story about two black teenagers and their experiences in Vietnam. The novel provides numerous points for later comparison with Remarque's novel: the soldiers' anticipation of going to battle; their horrifying experiences face-to-face with the enemy; their thoughts of life back home; the role of mothers and girlfriends in their lives; their conclusions about the meaning (and meaninglessness) of war.

- Harry Mazer's autobiographical novel *The Last Mission* provides students with the same kinds of insights—but regarding World War II, when a young airman is shot down over Czechoslovakia and then captured by German soldiers.

- Mazer's short story "Furlough 1944" (published in Donald Gallo, *Sixteen: Short Stories by Outstanding Writers for Young Adults*) shows the psychological preparation of a young soldier before going off to war.

- For a soldier's view of the horrors of war, your class can examine Wilfred Owens's poem "Dulce Et Decorum Est" about being gassed during World War I (it can be found in various anthologies), and Phil George's Native American perspective in "Battle Won Is Lost," found in *Zero Makes Me Hungry: A Collection of Poems for Today*.

- Additional perspectives of the Vietnam War can be found, among other sources, in Tim O'Brien's *The Things They Carried** and Ellen Emerson White's *The Road Home*, a historical novel about the effects of the war on a young nurse both during and after the war.

- For nonfictional accounts, students (especially males) appreciate *Bloods: An Oral History of the Vietnam War by Black Veterans** edited by Wallace Terry. Consider also *Dear America: Letters Home from Vietnam* edited by Bernard Edelman, and *Voices from Vietnam*, by Barry Denenberg—which include personal narratives from soldiers, political leaders, medical personnel, and journalists, including North Vietnamese as well as Americans.

- What happens to the people back home and to veterans after a war can be examined through a reading of Bobbie Ann Mason's *In Country*, a novel in which the 17-year-old female narrator's father has died in Vietnam and her "guardian" suffers from the effects of Agent Orange. Their visit to the Vietnam War Memorial—The Wall—is the culminating cathartic experience for them.

- For another perspective of The Wall, you can read aloud to your class the scene from Katherine Paterson's *Park's Quest* in which Park first visits the war memorial and locates his dead father's name there. Or examine selections from Thomas B. Allen's *Offerings at the Wall: Artifacts from the Vietnam Veterans Memorial Collection*, which describes some of the 25,000 items—photos, combat boots, medals, teddy bears—that have been left at The Wall.

- To get the maximum effect, read and show your class the illustrations from Eve Bunting's moving picture book *The Wall*.

- For a quiet conclusion, recite Carl Sandburg's poem "Grass," from *Harvest Poems*.

If you are interested in thematic approaches like this one for other major required works, we recommend a pair of particularly helpful books edited by Joan F. Kaywell: *Adolescent Literature as a Complement to the Classics*, Volumes 1 (1993) and 2 (1994).

RESTRUCTURING THE CLASSROOM

As former students, most of us who teach English and reading experienced only one way of teaching literature: one book at a time, studied usually for a three-week period. We call that a *unit*. Some of us, usually on our own, have learned the value of a thematic approach where the *ideas* are viewed as more important than the individual literary work. Instead of reading and discussing one book in excruciating detail, we examine more broadly two or more works that deal with the same theme or themes.

Teaching in this way, as you have no doubt noticed, requires not only a change in attitude but also modifications in class structure. You probably have been asking yourself: *If I can't get my students to read* Great Expectations *[or* Hamlet *or whatever] all the way through on their own to begin with, how am I supposed to get them to read* two *books for the same assignment? And where does the extra time come from to do that anyway?* Important questions! Here are some comments that will help you answer them.

Nobody ever has to force teenagers to go to a movie. They go because they know from experience that movies are interesting—or at least they go to movies that they have heard are interesting. They are attracted by the ads they see on television or by recommendations from their friends. The word around your school—if your school is like most other schools in this country—is that many, if not most, of the required books are not very interesting.

But when teachers select required books that most students can handle and do enjoy, then students are more likely to want to read other similar books. And if we constantly recommend all kinds of good books to our students, and if we provide time for the students in our classes to talk with others in class about good books they have read or are reading, we create a positive atmosphere that will carry over to the required reading.

In other words, if we prove to our students that we understand the kinds of books they are interested in reading, they will begin to trust our judgment about other books. Similarly, if the students in our classes have heard good things from older students about the books those students read in our previous classes, the students in our current classrooms will be more willing to read the books we require and recommend. And carefully chosen Young Adult novels and stories are those kinds of literary works.

So, if we introduce our students to exciting, readable, rewarding novels (and other types of literary works) from the start, they will be interested in reading them and will do so more willingly. After all, when we do something willingly and with a certain amount of personal interest in the activity, we are likely to do it more quickly and more competently than if we are not enthusiastic about the task. In addition, because YA novels are almost always shorter and easier to read than the complex, adult-oriented classics, our students will be able to finish the books in a much shorter amount of time than we normally set aside for the reading of a book that they will view as little more than drudgery. A week or two is sufficient time for most students to read and discuss the main issues in most YA books. (You can decide to spend more time—or less—on a book according to its length and complexity as well as the ability of students in that class and their level of interest and involvement.)

Print isn't the only useful "literature" we can recommend. Videos, audio recordings, and information from CD-ROM programs on the same themes should also be considered.

Within the traditional three-week unit, there are approximately two weeks to examine the classic that will follow. How can we manage the former three weeks of readings and assignments in only two weeks?

First, because our students (we expect) have been so successful in reading and discussing the YA novel, theoretically they should be somewhat more interested in reading the classic—with the same themes and issues—than they otherwise might have been; and they therefore will read the book with greater commitment and, possibly, with greater speed.

Second, because the class already will have examined the major themes and issues of the unit during discussion of the YA novel and other shorter selections, the students will have a focus when they read the more complex classic.

Third, because the specific themes and issues in the classic have already been identified, class activities and discussions should concentrate on those instead of on more picky elements. For example, the class can discuss the personalities and motivations of characters instead of recalling what they wore in Chapter 1. The class can examine the manner in which the protagonist deals with the moral dilemma in the classic and compare that with the manner in which the protagonist in the YA novel dealt with her or his dilemma. Big issues. Major themes. Not picky details, line by line, scene by scene, chapter by chapter.

Moreover, if you accept the value of helping students to become more responsible for their own learning—through self-selected goals, small-group assignments, cooperative learning activities, and the like—and your students have demonstrated their ability to do those things at least adequately during the reading of the YA novel, then those same students should be able to use the same skills to examine the classic in the same manner. Thus, *they* will decide which are the most important issues to discuss and explore, with you recommending others if the students have missed any you deem important. Daily quizzes on minor details, designed to punish (or embarrass) unprepared students and "motivate" recalcitrant readers will not be necessary. (In fact, if you have discovered the value of response journals—in which students write their personal reactions to the literature as they read—you will already have eliminated pop quizzes.)

Remember, our goal is to help students find pleasure in reading and to make them life-long readers. Using YA novels and other shorter works as bridges to the classics or to other required literature will help us achieve that goal. Once you get over the insecurity of doing something so different, you'll see how much more involved your students are in their work, how much more they enjoy it, and how much more they are learning. And you are likely to discover an excitement about teaching that you haven't felt in years.

Chapter 5

CREATING LIBRARY LIONS

Lions usually travel in packs, finding and sharing a space. And so do many adolescents. Thus, creating a new library space that caters exclusively to their pack instinct might be a way to entice adolescents to become library users.

Why bother? If we really want students to become lifetime readers, then we have to change their image of libraries. And teachers, library/media specialists, and public librarians need to develop a collaborative relationship to convince students to become browsers and shoppers at libraries, in the way that they browse and shop at malls. To reach this goal, we have to convince teenagers to become "library lions"—to feel welcome and comfortable enough to visit with their pack, and to investigate the merchandise on the shelves. Wouldn't it be great if they poked through shelves of books in the same way they poke through CDs, sneakers, cosmetics, or clothing?

Unfortunately, many teenagers associate school libraries with study halls, special tutoring, teacher-directed research, a place for catching up on homework, or a spot to rest between assigned periods. How many students think their school library is also a place to read for pleasure? This is a tough question to answer.

Ideally, a school library should have a special corner with shelves of YA and adult books, so when students enter the library they *know* where they can find a wide assortment of books that meet their needs and interests, an area away from reference materials, computer terminals, and the circulation desk. And this space should encourage them to browse, to read, and to have lively discussions. It's a good idea for teachers and library/media specialists to work together in setting up this area, because classroom teachers can describe the reading space to their students and schedule an introductory visit during a class period. Teachers and library/media specialists working together present a united front to students; thus, the reading area has credibility and students realize the library is more than an escape from study halls, unassigned periods, or cancelled classes.

PROMOTING YOUNG ADULT BOOKS IN SCHOOLS

YA books have to be promoted by both teachers and library/media specialists. Cheryl Karp Ward, library/media specialist at the Windsor Locks Middle School in Windsor Locks, Connecticut, uses two effective ways to promote YAL with students. She offers book and author talks and encourages teachers to schedule their class visits for specific periods during the school day, and she arranges exhibits of new and interesting books. One of the most popular displays in her media center is a shelf she labels as NEED TO KNOW, WANT TO KNOW, AFRAID TO ASK on which she places the latest self-help books as well as works of fiction about teenage problems: divorce, alcoholism, sexual abuse, physical handicaps, AIDS—topics that are crucial in any adolescent's life.

Ward tried an interesting strategy she heard about at a National Council of Teachers of English workshop presented by Dr. Kylene Beers of the University of Houston. Beers, who conducted research into the reading habits and attitudes of different kinds of readers in the seventh grade, recommended limiting the choice of books for what she terms *uncommitted readers* (i.e., students who do not usually enjoy reading and do not read much, but are still capable of reading). Beers noted that these students have difficulty choosing a book when left to browse through the entire collection. But if there is a *limited* choice—perhaps a box labeled GOOD BOOKS, TOO GOOD TO MISS, PAGE TURNERS, or the like—these uncommitted readers could look at the titles and choose one easily. Ward reports that this strategy has worked well with these types of readers in her school.

Another library/media specialist who promotes all kinds of books with teachers and students is Harriet Selverstone, department chair, Library/Media Specialists, Norwalk Public Schools, Norwalk, Connecticut. Selverstone is assigned to Norwalk High School, where she has created innovative programs to attract students and teachers to the media center. She coordinates a "Reading Assembly" at which guests read excerpts from essays, novels, or poems around a theme, such as "Readers Are Leaders." Every week she includes a short review of two new books in the weekly schedule that is circulated to teachers and students, and invariably a teacher or student checks these titles out by the time the schedule is posted. She also works with classroom teachers, filling their requests for particular genres for their English classes, and she booktalks many of the titles when the class meets in the media center. She maintains a special collection of specially marked high interest/low reading level books for Communication Skills classes, but she catalogs them with the regular collection so that students feel comfortable selecting any book from the shelves. She displays different groups of softcover books in "comfortable" areas of the library where students can browse through titles, and she asks students which books they like so she can update her book displays. For a special program on AIDS, she received a cooperative grant from the Southern Connecticut Library Council and set up an exhibit of books to tie in with the Improvisational Theatre Group that performed in the evening. In addition, she arranged for the ninth grade teaching team to visit the reference librarian at the Norwalk Public Library after school so they could familiarize themselves with the electronic resources available for their students who were participating in a special interdisciplinary unit, "Science and Society." Also for the ninth grade team, she compiled an annotated bibliography of fiction and nonfiction and shared all curriculum materials and bibliographies with the reference librarian at the public library.

A successful high school English program that integrates YAL with the required curriculum was created at O. H. Platt High School in Meriden, Connecticut, by Carol H. Davidson, library/media specialist, and Sandra Klimkowski, integrated language arts teacher. Because these teachers believe their program might be the last chance for many of their students to become involved in reading, they subtly infuse YAL as supplemental reading along with the required classics. At the beginning of the school year Davidson, who spends every summer catching up on the latest in YAL paperbacks, booktalks the best YAL with Klimkowski's ninth and tenth graders. Students are required to select one of the new titles and to present an oral or visual report about the novel, as well as some information about the author. Both teachers believe this first assignment familiarizes students with quality YAL and prepares them for supplemental readings that are listed in various theme units.

For example, if the required novel is John Knowles's *A Separate Peace*, Davidson and Klimkowski have developed a group of supplemental readings around the theme "Youth in War." They offer YAL such as *Fallen Angels* by Walter Dean Myers or *The Last Mission* by Harry Mazer, along with *April Morning* by Howard Fast or *All Quiet on the Western Front* by Erich Maria Remarque. Students maintain journals on these readings, and both teachers read and respond to the students' journals. Over the course of the school year as the classes meet in the library to select books, most students are reading YAL along with the classics, and many students are becoming enthusiastic readers. In some instances, when students are excited and impressed by a particular title, that book might be adopted as a new title for the English classes.

Harriet Selverstone, Cheryl Ward, Carol Davidson, and Sandra Klim-kowski are but a few examples of proactive school library/media special-ists and teachers who use their imagination and ingenuity to engage students so they become library readers. By collaborating with other teachers and students, they validate the possibilities for creating a positive reading environment in schools.

PUBLIC LIBRARY PROGRAMS

Public libraries should reflect the same concern about the needs of adolescent readers. Most teenagers use public libraries for research, particularly to access information that is not available in their school library. In many instances, public libraries have a children's section that includes materials for prekindergarten through sixth or seventh grade; the rest of the fiction and informational materials are catalogued for other library users, which could include adolescents, college students, adults, or any age group. But where are the YA books and other informational materials specifically published for teenagers? And how do teenagers begin to look for these reading materials if there is no identifiable YA section? How can librarians and school library/media specialists make these facilities more user-friendly? By convincing students that school and public libraries exist for their social and intellectual needs; that there are shelves of books set aside for them, along with the general collection; and by persuading them that they are valued clients.

Many exemplary programs in schools and libraries are described in professional journals such as *School Library Journal* and *Voice of Youth Advocates*. However, there are common themes that appear again and again: the success of any library program is dependent on student involvement in planning the space, on maintaining the collection, and on planning special activities.

In the October 1994 issue of *Voice of Youth Advocates* entitled "For Young Adults Only: Tried and True Youth Participation Manual," Leila J. Sprince, head of Youth Services, Broward County West Regional Library, Planta-tion, Florida, describes a multidimensional program for young adult volunteers. The program involves them in working with the professional staff in many areas, such as shelving books, setting up rooms for craft programs, processing new books, assisting in the children's room, and helping patrons. The Teen Volunteer Recruitment Program enables teen-agers to gain job experience, to receive a community service award upon graduation from high school, and to establish a constructive relationship with other young people. Some of these volunteers are invited to join a

Young Adult Advisory Board. As members of the board they begin to plan recreational, information-service, and book-related programs for other local teens. Obviously these teens will have strong ties to the library as they directly participate in decision making that affects their peers.

The Arlington, Virginia, library has a Teen Advisory Board (TAB, also an acronym for Teens Are Beneficial) that reads, reviews, and presents booktalks in cooperation with the town's four middle schools. Over one hundred students read and review books for the library, and publishers send advance copies for reviewing prior to publication. Many of these students are bonded to the library and continue to volunteer or work at the library during their high school years (Brown and Muller, 1994).

A unique outreach program for teenagers was implemented in Berkeley, California, through a grant from the California State Library, by Kay Finney, reference and Young Adult librarian at the South Branch Library. In her article in the April 1994 issue of *Voice of Youth Advocates*, Finney asks an important question: "Want to honor your mandate to serve historically neglected constituencies?" She describes a program that trains at-risk high school students to work in all phases of the library program, particularly in helping the staff to plan interesting activities that will attract teenagers. Again, the teenagers gain job experience with adults and the public; and as Finney points out, by working in the building "they help us break down the widespread stereotype that 'library' means 'old, white, boring, irrelevant' " (1994, 14). This program has garnered community support through the success of the high school students' suggested programming, such as a Rap and Poetry Jam, a neighborhood health fair, and other activities that bring young people to the various library branches.

SCHOOL AND PUBLIC LIBRARY COOPERATION

Probably the most important factor in any successful program is cooperation and communication between school and public library/media specialists working with teachers. It is important for these professionals to maintain an ongoing dialogue in order to stimulate students' reading habits. Some common ground that both libraries could establish includes:

- maintaining current school curriculum guides
- visiting with students to inform them about new resources in the public library to meet their special needs
- inviting public library youth services staff to visit schools to present booktalks on special topics for teachers and students
- establishing and maintaining an electronic network among schools and public libraries
- sharing professional development goals

- developing bibliographic instruction for particular school assignments
- maintaining reserve shelves for particular school assignments
- assisting each other in developing annotated lists for summer and special reading programs.

By working together closely, these professionals can begin to assess what works so that both school and public library reading spaces lure teenage readers. There should be shelves of "too good to miss" books, along with a special place for teenagers—*their* space—where they can talk about reading, whether criticizing, recommending, or browsing. Could going to the library compete with going to the mall?

THE COMFORT FACTOR

And *welcome* is the operative word here. As students use the reading area, they will begin to feel comfortable and enjoy the collection. They will spread the word so that more students begin to use the reading space—their books, their chairs, their couches, their shelves—where they can talk and argue and get excited about books; where they can be themselves, discussing books just as they discuss music, clothes, parties, and friends. And an important part of this exchange is learning from each other, listening to each other, and learning to respect each other's opinion. After all, where else can teenagers have a space to sit around and discuss a book that is not assigned and analyzed by teachers? We realize there might be less talk about books and more socializing, rowdy behavior, and loud voices; but if we want students to enjoy reading, then don't we have to convince them that reading is not confined to a classroom assignment? A little experimentation will help us find the best ways to motivate our students to use school and public libraries for unassigned, pleasurable reading. The key ingredient, of course, is having a good collection of YA books, fiction, nonfiction, plays, poetry, drama, biography, books based on current films, all kinds of books. And magazines too.

School and public libraries might want to woo teenagers with a special bulletin board in the reading area that features book or CD reviews; includes career and/or college catalogs; offers homework support or tutoring service; and lists community teen activities, job and volunteer information, training in baby sitting, emergency medical techniques, or library reference work so that the area becomes a teenage community resource.

An exemplary program for teenage involvement in a public library was started in 1987 by Barbara Blosveren, Young Adult Services department head of the Stratford Library Association in Stratford, Connecticut. This award-winning program still flourishes and grows because Blosveren and her staff provide an atmosphere of inclusion for young adults, as well as an innovative and diverse program that caters to the needs and interests of teenage users. A member of the Young Adult Services Department is available at all times for teenagers. The department has a Homework Desk for students, a separate Reference Desk so that students won't be intimidated but will feel free to ask any question, a Young Critics Club, and a Stratford Youth Review Board that compiles an annotated bibliography—the *Gold Seal Booklist*—printed and distributed annually. (Recently the Youth Review Board printed a five-year collection of recommended titles for young adults; more than 70 board members contributed to the list of 135 titles.) Also, a Youth Participation Group involves 50 teenagers who participate in two orientation sessions before they can volunteer to perform plays, handle story hours, and assist in craft programs for young children. A Teen Women's Support Group recently scheduled eight evening sessions of peer counseling and aerobics and attracted 25 participants. The success of this program is evident in Blosveren's commitment to young adults.

In a recent interview, she mentioned that although senior high students get jobs and leave the Youth Review Board, they still make time to volunteer at the annual book sale and still stop at the Young Adult Services desk because of their past participation in the Stratford Library Youth Review Board. These young adults obviously *feel* connected to their public library.

Blosveren also works with Philip Devine, supervisor of language arts, K–12, for the Stratford, Connecticut School District. She helps coordinate the school district's required summer reading program with Devine so that annotated book lists and books are grouped prominently in various parts of the public library's YA section for various grade levels. If a teacher calls her with a request for books related to a specific theme or genre, she will have these books available when students come to the Stratford Library. Stratford teachers and students know that Barbara Blosveren's dedication to young readers makes the library *their* special place.

Establishing a student advisory panel in a school or a public library is a positive way for librarians and library/media specialists to bring young adults into the library. These volunteers can feel they are a part of the library by doing any of the following:

- assisting other readers in making book selections
- helping decide which materials to purchase for the YA collection
- writing book reviews for school and local newspapers
- compiling annotated bibliographies
- developing summer reading lists
- volunteering to booktalk titles at the library or in classrooms
- helping teachers select titles and maintain classroom collections.

As the teen advisory panel becomes entrenched in the media center of the school, it changes the atmosphere so that more students are attracted to books and other informational materials.

And this teen advisory panel could become a recognized extracurricular activity. For example, it could promote an outreach program at elementary libraries by organizing story hours, dramatic programs, and booktalks for young students. Some members of the panel might want to lead book discussion groups at a local senior citizen center or organize a bookmobile for shut-ins. They could organize exhibits and displays with the library/media specialist and help organize forums or speakers for Women's History Month, Censorship Week, African-American History Month, and other subjects related to health, education, and social needs in the community. They could serve as a liaison with public librarians concerning programs at school. By doing so, these young people will learn important skills for their future careers: working with a wide range of age groups, servicing the public, implementing and organizing programs in and out of school, and most important, learning to cooperate and use their initiative with peers and professional staff members. And, of course, all these activities will look impressive on their job or college applications.

As the student advisory panel becomes more involved in making decisions about youth services programs with the professional staff, the more successful the reading program will become. Certainly, circulation figures could be one means of assessment.

One other suggestion. If space permits, the adolescent reading area at the public library should be away from the children's section. After all, teenagers are at a stage where they move back and forth between YA books and the classics, and they might also occasionally dip into a "best seller" adult book. It's a good idea to find a *neutral* space for these eclectic readers. And, because many students prefer softcover books, the collection should consist of paperbacks whenever possible.

Library/media specialists and teachers working together are the cornerstone of any reading program for adolescents. The library/media specialists' expertise and knowledge about informational and fiction books, along with electronic informational services, and the teachers' experience with students' idiosyncratic reading habits, create a strong partnership to ensure enthusiastic readers.

Chapter 6

OTHER BACKYARDS: USING YOUNG ADULT BOOKS FOR INTERDISCIPLINARY STUDIES

Young Adult Literature complements other disciplines and affords teachers an opportunity to introduce students to novels related to other subject areas. In fact, a wide selection of titles can dovetail into many of the concepts introduced in subject areas such as social studies, physical education, art, music, science, health, and the humanities.

It is not unusual for English teachers and social studies teachers to share the same group of students in a humanities program. Many English and social studies classes are linked around American history and literature; this is a good fit whereby students have the opportunity to read literature that reflects a particular historical era. But what happens when a student reaches an impasse? What if the student cannot integrate Hawthorne's *The Scarlet Letter* with his or her understanding of the Puritans in Salem, Massachusetts, during the 1600s? Depending on the assignment and the expectations of the humanities team, wouldn't it be a good idea to provide more accessible titles to students who need to ease into the Puritan era with a less demanding book—one that includes many of the historical characteristics they can recognize easily?

Usually there is only one text for a history class, with some supplementary material; English teachers, however, have the luxury of clustering biography, poetry, drama, and fiction around a historical period. In a humanities class, where there are students of varying reading ability, it makes sense to offer alternatives to the prescribed text. Who knows? After reading a YA novel about witchcraft in Salem, Massachusetts, students might be willing to tackle *The Scarlet Letter* later.

But history or social studies classes aren't the only areas in which Young Adult Literature can reinforce major ideas. Many YA titles tie into other disciplines as well. And because these books are accessible to all levels of readers, teachers could assign them as outside reading. For example, the science and English teachers might plan a reading/writing assignment around an ecology unit. Wouldn't the study of ecology in a science class come alive and become more meaningful when students select novels that portray characters involved in an ecology-related situation? After selecting from a wide array of titles, both YA and adult novels, the teachers could ask some reader/response questions that could help students to think about the factual information they observe and discuss in science class and consider how this knowledge is reflected in the fiction they are reading.

As they switch back and forth between scientific reading and fictional reading for language arts, the students become more discriminating readers. For example, many readers begin to notice the author's use of ecological information in character and plot development. On the basis of their scientific knowledge, some students can determine if the author's information in the novel is authentic or believable. Reader/response questions can require students to refer to the ecology concepts introduced in the science class in analyzing and interpreting the novel. The students will receive reading credit in both subject areas; both teachers can evaluate students' responses to the assignment. Book discussion among students could be scheduled during the language arts period, and a final essay could be assigned by the two teachers.

Another advantage to the integration between reading/language arts and various disciplines is the message students receive about the importance of reading across the curriculum. This isn't spouting litany; this is acting on one's beliefs. After all, reading and writing are not the exclusive purview of English/language arts teachers. *All* teachers are responsible for helping students learn, and students learn by becoming independent readers. Also, by working with teachers of other disciplines we emphasize the importance of collegiality, the opportunity to understand a variety of approaches to a discipline. The advantage of introducing YA titles is obvious: as mentioned in Chapter 1, YA novels have protagonists who are teenagers; the books are short enough for most students to read outside the classroom; and there are enough choices in YAL to meet any student's ability level.

A couple of years ago a high school teacher called me at home at 10 P.M., sounding frustrated. A group of girls in his tenth grade American History class were driving him crazy—they didn't listen, didn't hand in any work, and said they were bored. The class was studying the development of the New England mills around Lowell, Massachusetts. He needed a "hot" novel that these girls could read. He was lucky—I had just read *Lyddie* by

Katherine Paterson. Talk about a perfect fit! I sent him a list of other historical novels they could read as well, and later he said their attitude had changed. He now uses several different historical novels to complement his American History textbook.

I had a similar experience with a Health and Family Life teacher who teaches seventh and eighth graders. Her courses cover nutrition, substance abuse, AIDS, sexuality, physical development, and related topics. We talked about YAL she could use as outside reading assignments and how we could collaborate so that students could receive credit in both English and Health and Family Life classes.

The possibilities are unlimited, depending on the imagination and commitment of colleagues. Here are some representative YA titles in several content areas. This list is only selective and not exhaustive. *Remember: titles that deal with multicultural themes or issues are followed by an asterisk (*).*

ART

Cole, Brock. *Celine*. Sixteen-year-old Celine uses her artistic talent to deal with parental neglect.

Oneal, Zibby. *In Summer Light*. A talented girl lives in the shadow of her artist father.

_____ . *The Language of Goldfish*. Drawing helps a teenager deal with her mental problems.

Peck, Richard. *Unfinished Portrait of Jessica*. Jessica's uncle is a talented painter who helps her.

DANCE

Williams-Garcia, Rita. *Blue Tights*.* Joyce discovers her black heritage with an African dance group.

HEALTH

Arrick, Fran. *What You Don't Know Can Kill You*. An older teenager discovers she is HIV-positive because of her boyfriend's indiscretion.

Doherty, Berlie. *Dear Nobody*. Chris and Helen learn about love and separation when she becomes pregnant.

Kerr, M. E. *Night Kites*. A young boy's family collapses when they find out his older brother has AIDS.

Levenkron, Steven. *The Best Little Girl in the World*. A young girl nearly dies battling anorexia.

Levy, Marilyn. *Rumors and Whispers*. A teenager deals with her brother's homosexual lifestyle.

Mazer, Norma Fox. *Out of Control.* Valerie has the courage to accuse three popular males in her high school of sexual harassment.

Voigt, Cynthia. *When She Hollers.* Tish suffers the lies in her family life until she confronts her stepfather.

A comprehensive guide to a variety of health-related issues for adolescents, complete with annotated bibliography, is available in *Adolescents at Risk* (1993, 1994), a guide to fiction and nonfiction for young adults, parents, and professionals, edited by Joan F. Kaywell.

HISTORY/SOCIAL STUDIES/HUMANITIES

Middle Ages

Cushman, Karen. *Catherine, Called Birdy.* The diary of a 14-year-old daughter of an English nobleman in 1290.

———. *The Midwife's Apprentice.* The story of a nameless, homeless girl in the fourteenth century who becomes the apprentice of a midwife.

McKinley, Robin. *The Hero and the Crown.* A fantasy about Aerin, who proves herself by slaying dragons and defending her country.

Pierce, Tamara. The Lioness Quartet: *Alanna; In the Hands of the Goddess; The Woman Who Rides Like a Man;* and *Lioness Rampant.* Alanna of Trebond hides her identity, becomes a knight, and proves her courage and physical prowess.

Vining, Elizabeth Gray. *Adam of the Road.* A wandering minstrel's life in thirteenth-century England.

American History

Early America

Clapp, Patricia. *Witches' Children: A Story of Salem.* Mary Warren reveals the truth about the accusers.

Fleischman, Paul. *Saturnalia.** William, a Native American captive, describes life in Boston in 1681.

Petry, Ann. *Tituba of Salem Village.** A description of Tituba's treatment when she is accused of witchcraft.

Rinaldi, Ann. *A Break with Charity.* Susanna knows the truth about the accusers but is sworn to secrecy in order to protect her family.

Revolutionary War

Fast, Howard. *The Hessian.* A Hessian drummer boy finds sanctuary with a Quaker family after an attack by the militia.

O'Dell, Scott. *Sarah Bishop.* The story of a young woman whose family is divided during the War for Independence.

Rinaldi, Ann. *A Stitch in Time.* Set in Salem, Massachusetts, in 1788, this is the story of the Chelmsford family during and after the war.

Slavery

Fox, Paula. *The Slave Dancer.** A young musician is kidnapped and forced to play music on a slave ship.

Hamilton, Virginia. *Many Thousand Gone: African Americans from Slavery to Freedom.** Individual histories of slaves' experiences.

McKissick, Patricia C., and Frederick McKissick. *Sojourner Truth: Ain't I A Woman?** The biography of a slave who became a spokesperson against slavery and for women's suffrage.

Paulsen, Gary. *Nightjohn.** Sarny learns to read and write from Nightjohn despite threats by her master. Based on archival material.

Rinaldi, Ann. *Wolf by the Ears.** Is Harriet Hemmings, daughter of the slave Sally, Thomas Jefferson's daughter?

Westward Movement

Hudson, Jan. *Sweetgrass.** Suffering from starvation and smallpox, a Blackfoot Indian tribe comes to depend on the skills of a 15-year-old girl for their survival.

Lasky, Kathryn. *Beyond the Divide.** An Amish girl travels with her father to California during the Gold Rush and learns to survive.

Paulsen, Gary. *Mr. Tucket.** Francis Tucket travels in a wagon train to Oregon and is captured by the Pawnees.

Yep, Laurence. *Dragon's Gate.** A Chinese boy joins his father and others digging a tunnel for the transcontinental railroad through the Sierra Nevada mountains in 1867.

Civil War

Foote, Shelby. *Shiloh.** A fictitious view of the Civil War narrated by three soldiers from the North and three soldiers from the South.

Hansen, Joyce. *Which Way Freedom?** The story of a slave, Obi, who is sold and separated from his family.

———. *Out from This Place.** Obi's family tries to reunite after the Civil War.

Murphy, Jim. *The Long Road to Gettysburg.* Authentic journals of two young soldiers engaged in the battle, with maps, photographs, and paintings.

Rinaldi, Ann. *In My Father's House.** A young girl observes the disintegration of southern plantation life during the war.

———. *The Last Silk Dress.* Susan Chilmark wants to support the Confederacy, but after nursing the wounded she rejects the war.

Great Depression

Hunt, Irene. *No Promises in the Wind.* Two young boys leave home and search for work in the Midwest.

Peck, Robert Newton. *Arly*.* Arly Poole, son of a migrant worker, escapes Jailtown with the help of a schoolteacher.

_____ . *A Day No Pigs Would Die*. Rob has to take charge of the family after his father dies.

_____ . *A Part of the Sky*. After losing the farm, Rob keeps the family united.

World War II

Houston, Jean Wakatsuki, and James D. Houston. *Farewell to Manzanar*.* A young Japanese girl's remembrance of life in an internment camp in the United States.

Salisbury, Graham. *Under the Blood-Red Sun*.* A Japanese boy's life changes drastically after the bombing of Pearl Harbor in 1941.

Uchida, Yoshiko. *The Invisible Thread*.* Life in a Japanese internment camp in Utah.

Race/Civil Rights

Krisher, Trudy. *Spite Fences*.* A poor white southern girl's view of the civil rights movement.

Levine, Ellen. *Freedom's Children: Young Civil Rights Activists Tell Their Own Stories*.* A series of interviews with adults who were teenage activists during the Montgomery boycotts, Little Rock desegregation of schools, and other episodes.

Parks, Rosa. *Rosa Parks: My Story*.* An autobiographical account of the racial bigotry and segregation that permeated the South.

Walter, Mildred Pitts. *The Girl on the Outside*.* Two young Southerners are caught up in the desegregation of Little Rock schools.

Vietnam War

Ashabranner, Brent. *Always to Remember*. The story of the Vietnam War Memorial in Washington, D.C.

Edelman, Bernard, ed. *Dear America: Letters Home from Vietnam*. An examination of the spiritual and physical wounds as expressed in letters from soldiers, nurses, and Red Cross workers.

Goldman, Peter, and Tony Fuller. *Charlie Company: What Vietnam Did to Us*.* Veterans describe their suffering after the war.

Jenson, Kathryn. *Pocket Change*. A teenager tries to help her father, a Vietnam veteran, deal with his nightmares.

Mason, Bobbie Ann. *In Country*. A young girl travels to the memorial in Washington to touch her father's name inscribed on the wall.

Myers, Walter Dean. *Fallen Angels*.* Richie and his buddies are disillusioned about their army duty in Vietnam.

Palmer, Laura. *Shrapnel in the Heart: Letters and Remembrances from the Vietnam Memorial*. A description of the families, friends, and loved ones who leave remembrances at the memorial wall.

Paterson, Katherine. *Park's Quest.* After seeing his father's name on the memorial wall, a young boy visits his grandfather to find out about his dead father.

Paulsen, Gary. *The Crossing.** Manny, a young Mexican boy, befriends a Vietnam vet hoping he will take Manny across the border to Texas.

Talbert, Marc. *The Purple Heart.* Luke finds it difficult to establish a relationship with his disturbed father, a Vietnam vet.

Terry, Wallace. *Bloods.** Personal stories of black Vietnam vets.

Holocaust

Appleman-Jurman, Alicia. *Alicia: My Story.* An autobiographical account of Nazi atrocities.

Frank, Anne. *The Diary of a Young Girl.* A poignant memoir of a teenager's idealism while the Nazi regime destroys the Dutch Jews.

Gies, Miep, and Alison Leslie Gold. *Anne Frank Remembered.* The story of the woman who had the courage to hide and help the Frank family and retrieved Anne's diary.

Lowry, Lois. *Number the Stars.* A Danish family hides Jews and helps them escape.

Matas, Carol. *Daniel's Story.* Snapshot views of a boy's experiences during the Holocaust.

Rogasky, Barbara. *Smoke and Ashes: The Story of the Holocaust.* Graphic photographs show the extermination of Jews before and during World War II.

Sendar, Ruth. *The Cage.* A young Polish girl saves her younger siblings during their internment.

Siegel, Aranka. *Upon the Head of a Goat.* Piri, a 13-year-old Hungarian Jew, describes her life before the invasion of Hungary and her journey to Auschwitz.

Spiegelman, Art. *Maus: A Survivor's Tale.* A cartoonist's version of his father's survival tactics during the Holocaust.

Yolen, Jane. *Briar Rose.* After listening to her grandmother's story of The Sleeping Beauty, Becca unearths the atrocities her grandmother suffered in Poland.

JOURNALISM

Asher, Sandy. *Summer Smith Begins.* A student runs into trouble after writing an article in the school newspaper.

Crutcher, Chris. *Staying Fat for Sarah Byrnes.* Two students start an underground paper and are threatened.

Malmgren, Dallin. *The Ninth Issue.* A high school newspaper is censored by the school administrator.

Mazer, Norma Fox, and Harry Mazer. *Bright Days, Stupid Nights.* Four teenagers are interns on a summer newspaper.

Tamar, Erika. *The Things I Did Last Summer.* A teenager's summer job on a newspaper teaches him about honest journalism.

Zindel, Paul. *Harry and Hortense at Hormone High.* Harry and Hortense write reviews for the school newspaper.

MUSIC

Brooks, Bruce. *Midnight Hour Encores.* Sibilance is a talented cellist who learns about 1960s music from her father.

Hentoff, Nat. *Jazz Country.* * A young white boy wants to become a jazz musician.

Strasser, Todd. *Rock 'n' Roll Nights.* The adventures of a teenage rock band.

Wolff, Virginia Euwer. *The Mozart Season.* A young violinist discovers her inner resources while preparing for a challenging competition.

PHYSICAL EDUCATION/SPORTS

Crutcher, Chris. *Chinese Handcuffs.* Dillon Hemingway refuses to be bullied by school authorities who threaten him.

———. *The Crazy Horse Electric Game.* * When he loses his athletic coordination, Willie leaves town to find acceptance elsewhere.

———. *Ironman.* While training for a triathlon, Bo Brewster analyzes his combative relationship with his father.

———. *Running Loose.* * Louie Banks sacrifices football and friendship for his personal code of ethics.

———. *Staying Fat for Sarah Byrnes.* Eric Calhoun, alias Moby, keeps eating to show his loyalty to Sarah Byrnes.

———. *Stotan!* * A four-person swim team trains rigorously for a state meet and learns about loyalty and honesty.

Davis, Terry. *If Rock and Roll Were a Machine.* Bert Bowden's rides on his Harley-Davidson help him to regain confidence in his athletic ability.

———. *Vision Quest.* Louden Swain uses competitive wrestling to help find himself.

Deuker, Carl. *On the Devil's Court.* Joe makes a pact with the devil to prove to his father that he is a talented basketball player.

Duder, Tessa. *In Lane Three Alex Archer.* A female swimmer from New Zealand trains for the Olympics.

Gallo, Donald R., ed. *Ultimate Sports.* * Short stories about males and females engaged in various sports.

Hoffius, Stephen. *Winners and Losers.* Curt takes his injured friend's place on the high school track team.

Klass, David. *Wrestling with Honor.* A teenage wrestler fails a mandatory drug test.

Lipsyte, Robert. *The Brave.** When Sonny Bear leaves the Indian reservation, he meets up with Alfred Brooks of the New York Police Department.

———. *The Chief.** Sonny Bear trains as a boxing contender.

———. *The Contender.** Alfred Brooks escapes the ghetto by training to be a boxer.

Lynch, Chris. *Iceman.* A violent hockey player takes out his frustration on friends and enemies.

———. *Shadowboxer.* An older brother tries to discourage his younger brother from becoming a boxer.

Miklowitz, Gloria D. *Anything to Win.* An examination of the effects of steroid use in high school sports.

Myers, Walter Dean. *Hoops.** A black basketball player struggles to maintain his integrity on and off the court.

Spinelli, Jerry. *There's a Girl in My Hammerlock.* A junior high school girl joins the boy's wrestling squad.

Voigt, Cynthia. *The Runner.** Bullet Timmerman uses running to escape from an oppressive father.

———. *Tell Me If the Lovers Are Losers.* Three friends in college try out for the girls' volleyball team.

Wells, Rosemary. *When No One Was Looking.* A suspenseful sports story about a champion tennis player and her friend.

PSYCHOLOGY/PARAPSYCHOLOGY

Crutcher, Chris. *Staying Fat for Sarah Byrnes.* Eric Calhoun helps Sarah Byrnes unlock her silence.

Davis, Jenny. *Sex Education.* Livvie and David's caring project for biology class ends in tragedy.

Mahy, Margaret. *The Changeover.* Laura "changes over" into a witch in order to save her young brother.

Marsden, John. *So Much to Tell You.* Marina's diary explains why she has been silent for one year.

Sleator, William. *The Boy Who Reversed Himself.** Omar teaches Laura how to go to the fourth dimension.

———. *House of Stairs.* A group of orphans experience Skinnerian conditioning.

———. *Strange Attractors.* A teenage boy travels into various time frames via chaos theory.

Sweeney, Joyce. *Shadow.* A 14-year-old girl is protected from evil by the spirit of her dead cat.

SCIENCE/NATURE/ECOLOGY

Ecology

Collier, James Lincoln. *When the Stars Begin to Fall.* A teenage boy discovers a local factory polluting the water.

Dickinson, Peter. *Eva.* A chimp with a human brain struggles to save her companions from extinction.

Hesse, Karen. *Phoenix Rising.* Nyle's peaceful life on a sheep farm is changed radically when a nuclear power plant contaminates the surrounding farms.

Klass, David. *California Blue.* A runner discovers a new butterfly species in a forest owned by a lumber company.

Lipsyte, Robert. *The Chemo Kid.* Two teenagers try to stop the pollution of the town's reservoir.

Miklowitz, Gloria D. *After the Bomb.* Life in a Los Angeles suburb is described following a nuclear bomb explosion.

O'Brien, Rober C. *Z for Zachariah.* The diary of a teenage survivor of a nuclear war.

Sleator, William. *Others See Us.* A teenager falls into a toxic waste dump and discovers he has ESP.

Spinelli, Jerry. *Night of the Whale.* A boy and his classmates try to save a pod of stranded whales.

Stevermer, Caroline. *River Rats.* After a nuclear holocaust, a group of young survivors travels up and down the Mississippi River and encounters dangerous characters.

Nature

Cottonwood, Joe. *Quake!* A fictional account of a family's experience during the 1993 Los Angeles earthquake.

George, Jean Craighead. *Julie of the Wolves.** An Eskimo girl's experiences living with a pack of wolves.

Hobbs, Will. *Beardance.** An Indian boy rescues two grizzly bear cubs in Colorado.

——— . *Changes in Latitude.* A young boy and his brother try to save sea turtles in Acapulco.

——— . *Downriver.** A group of teenagers survive a rafting journey on the Colorado River.

Chapter 7

WHAT'S NEXT: WHERE CAN I FIND MORE INFORMATION?

Keeping up with new books is always a problem. In their teaching, too many teachers rely almost exclusively on books they read and learned about in college courses. Even if the books you read in those courses were published during the year you took the course, they are obviously not recent books if you've been teaching for ten years or more. That's probably why, along with the great classics, books such as *The Outsiders*, *The Pigman*, *A Day No Pigs Would Die*, and *The Chocolate War* are often found on many schools' required reading lists—they are all great books, modern classics every one, but the most recent is more than 20 years old! Few schools teach any of the recent excellent novels, many of which have been mentioned throughout this text.

For example, published in the early 1990s were a number of novels worthy of being included in the required literature programs in grades 6 through 12. Among them are Will Hobbs's *Beardance*, Robert Lipsyte's *The Chief*, Chris Crutcher's *Ironman*, Lois Lowry's *The Giver*, Terry Davis's *If Rock and Roll Were a Machine*, Chris Lynch's *Iceman*, Virginia Euwer Wolff's *Make Lemonade*, Norma Fox Mazer's *Out of Control*, Trudy Krisher's *Spite Fences*, Carolyn Coman's *Tell Me Everything*, Virginia Hamilton's *Plain City*, Robert Cormier's *Tunes for Bears to Dance To*, Richard Peck's *Unfinished Portrait of Jessica*, Cynthia Voigt's *When She Hollers*, and numerous novels by Gary Paulsen, including *Nightjohn* and *Harris and Me*.

If you are like most teachers of English and reading, you've read few of those books. Possibly you haven't read any of them, even though you may have heard about them. And if you haven't looked through the sources of information about new books, it's possible you haven't even heard of most of those titles. Yet this is only a smattering of the literally *hundreds* of new books published *each year* for teenage readers.

How competent would a physician be who prescribed only medicines he or she had learned about in medical school 10 or 20 years earlier? How effective would your auto mechanic be if he didn't keep up with changes in automobile parts and electronic systems?

So how can you keep up? How can you stay informed about what's new and, especially, what's good in this rich field of books for young people?

STUDENTS

The best sources of information are probably your students themselves, especially those who are avid readers. They are even more likely than most teachers to go into bookstores or peruse the paperback racks in grocery stores and pharmacies. Consider the amount of time the average teenager spends at the local mall—there's usually at least one major book-selling chain there. If your town has a good library, that may be another place where a lot of teens hang out. Sure, they're often there to socialize, but they also check out books. So ask your students what they are reading, or what books are being passed around the school. Most likely you'll hear about the latest and hottest titles in some romance or horror series, or the most recent novel by Stephen King or Danielle Steele. But you'll also hear about other titles: mass-market books that are popular with adults as well as books written for teenagers.

If your school has a silent recreational reading time during which everyone is supposed to be reading something for a 15- or 20-minute period, take a close look at what your students are reading during that time. (If your school doesn't have such a time period set aside for pleasure reading, think about starting one.) Or, if you have the dubious pleasure of supervising a study hall, that's an excellent time to eyeball the reading materials that those captive students have taken out of their bookbags. Also, at the beginning of the semester or once or twice during the school year, you can distribute a brief questionnaire to your classes asking for information about your students' reading habits, interests, favorite authors, and most recent books read.

Knowing what students find interesting is only part of the job. You also have to be willing to read a couple of those books yourself. Usually, if you ask a student if the book she or he is reading is good, you'll get a shrug of the shoulders and an unenthusiastic "It's okay." But don't give up. Ask what the book is about and what, specifically, is good about it. If you happen to be familiar with the book, or with another book by the same author, a dialogue will usually develop between you and the students.

Another way to make contact with students is that if you are reading a book yourself during the silent reading period or study hall, some student will almost always ask you about it. If your book happens to look like something a teenager would ordinarily read, that's even better. They'll want to know why you're reading one of *their* books. That will likely be the beginning of another dialogue.

If your dialogues are anything like those we have had with students, sooner or later one of your students is going to ask you to trade books. They will want to read your book, and they will want you to read theirs. Good swap.

But what if you are teaching in a school where there are no free reading periods and no study halls, and it seems as if no one reads? Where can you find out about good books to introduce to your students so they *will* read?

CATALOGS

If you are a school library/media specialist, you should automatically be receiving catalogs from major publishers at least once a year. Many publishers update their catalogs twice a year, sometimes even more frequently. If you aren't on the mailing list of Avon Books, Bantam Doubleday Dell, HarperCollins, Harcourt Brace, Houghton Mifflin, Macmillan, Penguin, Scholastic, Simon and Schuster, or any of the dozen or so other companies that publish books for children and young adults, write them a request on your school's letterhead. Publishers' addresses are listed in *Books in Print*.

If you are a teacher who buys a lot of books for your department or your own classroom, the publishers mentioned in the previous paragraph will be happy to add you to their catalog mailing list. If not, ask to borrow those catalogs from your librarian, or ask her or him to be sure to pass them along to you when they are no longer needed in the library.

In addition to catalogs from publishing houses, catalogs from paperback distributors have extensive and helpful lists. Furthermore, most distributors list books by category. If you are interested in certain types of books (say, Native American literature or historical fiction) or a set of books on a specific theme (say, Adventure/Survival or Teenagers in Turmoil), those folks have already done much of your homework for you. The catalogs also feature certain new books that have become immediately popular, and they note books that have won awards for quality, such as the Newbery Medal or the Coretta Scott King Award. When you purchase class sets of books or a certain number of books, these companies give discounts of 20 or 30 percent, occasionally even more. The two largest and most popular distributors, according to most librarians and teachers, are (1) Baker and Taylor, and (2) Follett. You can reach them at

> Baker and Taylor
> 652 East Main Street
> P.O. Box 6920
> Bridgewater, NJ 08807-0920
> 1-800-775-1800
> Fax: 1-800-775-7480

> Follett Library Resources
> 4506 Northwest Highway
> Crystal Lake, IL 60014-7393
> 1-800-435-6170
> Fax: 1-800-853-5458

There are also smaller paperback distributors throughout the country. In Connecticut an excellent distributor in Hartford—H. P. Kopplemann Paperback Book Service—provides pre-packaged collections, teacher guides to specific books, and teacher resources. Educators visiting Hartford can tour Kopplemann's warehouse with a grocery cart, happily selecting books from the shelves and then browsing through the Teacher Store next door. For a catalog, contact

> H. P. Kopplemann, Inc.
> 140 Van Block Avenue
> P.O. Box 145
> Hartford, CT 06141-0145
> 1-800-243-7724 or 860-549-6210
> Fax: 860-293-0279

Some distributors, such as Sundance in Massachusetts, produce their own teaching materials. For a copy of Sundance products, contact

> Sundance
> P.O. Box 1326
> Newtown Road
> Littleton, MA 01460
> 1-800-343-8204
> Fax: 508-486-1053

Also check the distributors in your area. For a listing of distributors throughout the United States, contact

> Educational Paperback Association
> P.O. Box 1399
> East Hampton, NY 11937

If your school prefers paperback books with hard covers, the most popular sources are Perma-Bound and Econo-Clad. Each carries more than 15,000 titles. For a copy of their catalogs, write or call them at

Perma-Bound Books
Vandalia Road
Jacksonville, IL 62650
1-800-637-6581 or 217-243-5451
Fax: 1-800-551-1169

American Econo-Clad Services
P.O. Box 1777
Topeka, KS 66601
1-800-255-3502
Fax: 1-800-628-2410

STORES

Be sure to peruse the shelves of your local bookstores. However, it is ironic that many bookstores—or other types of stores that carry books, such as large grocery chains and pharmacies—are not especially good places to find good books for teenagers. Shelf space is limited, so most stores stock only those types of books that sell best. And light-weight books sell far better than serious ones do. As a result, you will likely find shelf upon shelf of teenage romances, Sweet Valley High stories, and teenage horror novels by R. L. Stine, Christopher Pike, and their imitators, but very few of the more serious, more substantive works by Cormier, Crutcher, Voigt, and others mentioned earlier. (The average Sweet Valley High book and the newest R. L. Stine book purportedly sell about 500,000 copies each, while the average, more substantive novels for young adults sell about 2,500 copies in hardcover and 30,000 in paperback editions.) In most quality bookstores the new Young Adult hardcover books take up only a few feet of shelf space, possibly a little more in some of the larger chains such as Borders and Barnes & Noble. Thus, although it is worthwhile to browse through the YA section of your local bookstore to see what's new, you'll learn a lot more by reading reviews of new books in professional journals.

JOURNALS

Admitting to personal bias here, we believe that the most useful publication for classroom teachers looking for good new books for teenagers is *The ALAN Review*. It's also the most for the money. None of the sources mentioned up to this point in this chapter require any money. From here on we get into cost. Indeed, if you purchase several journals—or obtain memberships in the professional organizations that publish some of those journals—you can spend quite a lot of money each year just for information. (Of course, if you are joining a professional organization— such as the National Council of Teachers of English or the American Library Association—you get much more than information for the cost of your membership. Nevertheless, financial outlay is always a concern for classroom teachers who are paying out of their own pockets.)

ALAN stands for the Assembly on Literature for Adolescents of the National Council of Teachers of English (NCTE). If you are a teacher who is interested in specializing in books for adolescents, this is *the* resource for you. Unless you intend to become an officer of ALAN, you can join this organization without being a member of the NCTE. *The ALAN Review*, published three times a year, contains eight pages of reviews of new books, four reviews to a page. In addition, each issue contains several articles by authors, educators, and librarians about using Young Adult Literature in classrooms. Also, don't ignore the publishers' ads in this journal, or in other journals noted below; they indicate what's new and noteworthy from the point of view of individual publishing companies. For member-ship/subscription, contact

ALAN/NCTE
1111 W. Kenyon Road
Urbana, IL 61801
$15 per year

If you are an English teacher with membership in the National Council of Teachers of English, you are already receiving eight issues of the *English Journal* each school year and know that just about every issue contains either reviews of Young Adult books or an article on some aspect of Young Adult Literature, with other articles in the journal occasionally focusing on books in this field. If you teach English and are not a member of NCTE, you ought to be. For membership/subscription, contact

English Journal
National Council of Teachers of English
1111 W. Kenyon Road
Urbana, IL 61801
$40 per year

New from the NCTE is *Voices from the Middle*, a journal specializing in books and teaching activities for middle schools. Each of the year's four issues contains a "clip and file" section of reviews of 16 books for middle-school students and teachers. For subscription, contact

Voices from the Middle
National Council of Teachers of English
1111 W. Kenyon Road

Urbana, IL 61801
$15 per year

Other educators interested in books for teenagers are reading teachers and supervisors in grades 6 through 12, many of whom are members of the International Reading Association (IRA). With membership in IRA comes the *Journal of Adolescent & Adult Literacy* (until 1995 called the *Journal of Reading*), published eight times during the school year. Most issues contain a column of reviews of books for adolescents. This journal is *the* source if you are a secondary school reading teacher or supervisor. For membership/subscription, contact

Journal of Adolescent & Adult Literacy
International Reading Association
800 Barksdale Road
P.O. Box 8139
Newark, DE 19714-8139
$38 per year

As *The ALAN Review* is related to the NCTE, the *SIGNAL Newsletter* is related to the International Reading Association. Under new editorship and with an expanded and livelier format, published three times a year by SIGNAL, the Special Interest Group—a Network on Adolescent Literature within the IRA, this journal features articles about Young Adult Literature, bibliographies, and reviews of new YA books. This is another bargain. For membership/subscription, contact

SIGNAL Membership
English Department
Radford University
Radford, VA 24142-6935
$10 per year / $25 for 3 years

Library/media specialists are more likely to obtain information about books from journals that, understandably, contain articles about library and media use. But all these sources provide valuable book reviews for classroom teachers as well. These journals have many similar features—including annotated reviews, articles, and bibliographies—even though their organizations are somewhat different and they each have a slightly different focus. Almost all deal with books for children and for adults, as well as for adolescents. Among the most popular are

Booklist
434 West Downer
Aurora, IL 60506
$60 per year (bi-weekly)

The Horn Book Magazine
11 Beacon Street
Boston, MA 02108
$35 per year (bi-monthly)

The Horn Book also publishes, semi-annually, the *Horn Book Guide*, a compilation of the best books from the previous six months. Same address as the *Magazine*—$50 per year / $60 combined rate for *Magazine* and *Guide*.

School Library Journal
P.O. Box 57559
Boulder, CO 80322-7559
$74.50 per year (monthly)

The *Bulletin of the Center for Children's Books* is another useful publication, although not as popular as those noted above. This publication can be ordered from

University of Illinois Press
Journals Division
1325 South Oak
Champaign, IL 61820
$29 per year (monthly)

The same is true of *KLIATT*, a Young Adult paperback book guide. This is the only source that reviews only paperbacks in the field.

KLIATT
33 Bay State Road
Wellesley, MA 02181
$36 per year (bi-monthly)

Two publications that are sometimes more critical in their reviews are *Kirkus Reviews* and *Publishers Weekly* (*PW*). They are also more expensive, so classroom teachers are more likely to search out these sources in their town libraries than to purchase either one themselves. As its name suggest, *PW* provides information about what's happening in publishing companies and in the world of publishing in general, things the average classroom teacher doesn't care much about. But if you do, and if you can afford the cost, contact

Kirkus Reviews
200 Park Avenue South
Suite 1118
New York, NY 10003-1543
$75 per year (bi-weekly)

Publishers Weekly
P.O. Box 6457

Torrance, CA 90504
$139 per year (weekly)

The *Journal of Youth Services in Libraries* is another publication directed at library/media specialists but of interest to teachers specializing in books for young adults. Containing very few book reviews, the strength of this journal is in its articles about the field of YA books and in its Top of the News section, which keeps readers up-to-date on book awards, new resources, and conferences. To order this publication sponsored by the Association for Library Services to Children (ALSC) and the Young Adult Library Services Association (YALSA) of the American Library Association, contact

Journal of Youth Services in Libraries
Membership Department
50 East Huron Street
Chicago, IL 60611
$40 per year (quarterly)
$20 with ALSC or YALSA membership

Helpful to teachers trying to make connections between books and classroom activities, *Book Links*, also from the American Library Association, is an excellent investment. Although it focuses more on books for children, middle-school teachers will find the bibliographies, teaching ideas, writing activities, and authors' comments particularly valuable.

Book Links
434 W. Downer Place
Aurora, IL 60506-9954
$20 per year (bi-monthly)

Of similar value to both elementary and middle-school language arts teachers is *The New Advocate*, a journal of articles as well as reviews of new books for children and adolescents.

The New Advocate
Christopher-Gordon Publishers, Inc.
480 Washington Street
Norwood, MA 02062
$27 per year (quarterly)

Focusing on publications relating to various cultural groups is the *MultiCultural Review*. Along with articles, bibliographies, and a teachers' column, each issue provides insightful annotations of new books (organized by subject area), videos, and reference materials for educators and librarians seeking to keep up with the latest multicultural sources. Order from

MultiCultural Review
Greenwood Publishing Group, Inc.
88 Post Road West
P.O. Box 5007
Westport, CT 06881-5007
$59 per year (quarterly)

Last, but not least, is *VOYA*—the *Voice of Youth Advocates*. Begun as a more lively alternative to the somewhat staid library journals, *VOYA* has maintained its commitment to reviewing—along with the usual good books—horror, science fiction, and fantasy novels that most other sources ignore. And, unlike all but the *Journal of Youth Services in Libraries*, *The ALAN Review*, and the *SIGNAL Newsletter*, *VOYA* focuses exclusively on books for teenage readers. All titles are rated by quality and popularity, along with an indication of grade level of interest.

Scarecrow Press
Dept. VOYA
52 Liberty Street
P.O. Box 4167
Metuchen, NJ 08840
$38.50 per year (bi-monthly)

BOOKS

Although any of the aforementioned journals can be of great value to teachers and librarians seeking information about new books, there are other sources that provide compilations of books categorized by themes. These make it easier for students as well as educators to locate recent titles on specific topics (perhaps ecology, or teenage sexuality, or physical handicaps) or specific genres (such as poetry).

Foremost among these types of publications are *Your Reading* and *Books for You*. New editions of both books are published about every three years by the National Council of Teachers of English (NCTE address is noted earlier in this chapter). *Your Reading* is for middle-school/junior high school students, and *Books for You* is for readers at the high school level. Each annotates 2,000 or more recent titles, categorized by genre and topic.

A similar annotated listing from the NCTE is *High Interest–Easy Reading*, describing recent books likely to be more readable by less able readers in junior and senior high schools.

The American Library Association (50 East Huron Street, Chicago, IL 60611) publishes several books that are primarily annotated bibliographies. Teachers will find them valuable for locating titles in specific categories. Among them are:

Books by African-American Authors and Illustrators for Children and Young Adults by Helen E. Williams (1991) lists books published during the twentieth century, up to 1990.

The Best Years of Their Lives: A Resource guide for Teenagers in Crisis by Stephanie Zvirin (1992) is a self-help guide to 200 nonfiction books as well as novels and videos by category, including family matters, sexuality, and school problems.

Genre Favorites for Young Adults by Sally Estes (1993) contains information about books on subjects popular with teenagers, including mysteries, romance, humor, fantasy, and survival.

Against Borders: Promoting Books for a Multicultural World by Hazel Rochman (1993) includes chapters on such themes as The Perilous Journey, Friends and Enemies, and Family Matters, along with annotated lists of books by and about African Americans, Asian Americans, Jewish Americans, Latinos, and Native Americans.

Growing Up Is Hard to Do by Sally Estes (1994) reviews YA books under the categories of Growing Up Male, Growing Up Female, Growing Up in World War II, Growing Up Gay, Growing Up Religious, and so on.

Best Books for Young Adults by Betty Carter (1994) is another useful source for teachers and students seeking lists of award-winning books for young adults. Carter first describes the history of and issues involved in selecting the best books for young adults. Then she reproduces the complete, annotated lists of the best books from 1966 through 1993, both by author and by year, concluding with the Best of the Best lists from 1960–1974, 1970–1983, and 1966–1986.

Several commercial companies also have published books that contain extensive bibliographies of books for teenage readers. Among them (in no particular order) are:

Best Books for Junior High Readers, edited by John T. Gillespie (R. R. Bowker, 1991), contains over 5,000 annotated entries by category with a subject/grade level index.

Collected Perspectives: Choosing and Using Books for the Classroom, 2nd ed., edited by Hughes Moir (Christopher Gordon Publishers, 1992), reviews books for children as well as young adults. It includes recommended grade levels and annotations, along with teaching and writing topics and related books on each theme.

Adolescents at Risk: A Guide to Fiction and Nonfiction for Young Adults, Parents, and Professionals by Joan F. Kaywell (Greenwood Press, 1993) lists fiction and nonfiction books in several categories, including Adopted and Foster Families, Alcohol and Drugs, Eating Disorders, Teenage Pregnancy, and Suicide, with related articles on each subject.

Recreating the Past: A Guide to American and World Historical Fiction for Children and Young Adults by Lynda G. Adamson (Greenwood Press, 1994) provides annotations of 970 books appropriate for grades 1 through 10, organized by geographical place (e.g., the American Colonies, India, Vietnam) and time period (e.g., 1861–1865). Among several appendices are ones on readability and interest levels of the selections, famous groups and people, and specific settings of books in Europe and the British Isles.

This Land Is Our Land: A Guide to Multicultural Literature for Children and Young Adults by Althea K. Helbig and Agnes Regan Perkins (Greenwood Press, 1994) examines 559 titles published between 1985 and 1993 and gives information about other older and recent titles by the same authors. Books are grouped by ethnicity (African, Asian, Hispanic, and Native American) as well as by genre (fiction, oral tradition, poetry) within each ethnic grouping. Titles are also grouped by subject and grade level.

What Do Young Adults Read Next? A Reader's Guide to Fiction for Young Adults by Pam Spencer (Gale Research, 1994). This comprehensive analysis of 1,500 books published between 1988 and 1992, with additional suggestions of older works, notes the topics, themes, major characters, location, time period, and basic plot for each selection, along with major works by each author and recommended age range. The cross-referenced index is an additional asset.

Also helpful for classroom teachers is *A Thematic Guide to Young Adult Literature— Annotations, Critiques and Sources* by Kay Parks Bushman (The Writing Conference, Inc., 1993). Packaged in a three-ring notebook, each entry includes a listing of the strengths of each literary work along with recommended grade level use.

The Fall 1993 issue of the *Connecticut English Journal*, although not literally a book, has all the characteristics of one, being 170 pages long. Guest-edited by Don Gallo and titled *Literature for Teenagers: New Books, New Approaches* (available from the National Council of Teachers of English), this issue contains 27 articles by many of the best educators in the field (among them Leila Christenbury, Ted Hipple, Betty Poe, and M. Jerry Weiss) and an additional 10 by authors of Young Adult books (including Sandy Asher, Bette Greene, Harry Mazer, and Joan Lowery Nixon).

BOOK AWARDS

Lists of award-winning books are always worth examining, although readers need to be aware of the selection criteria: were the books chosen for their literary quality (as the Newbery Medal books always are) or for their potential interest to teenagers as well as for their literary quality (as the Best Books for Young Adults are)? In either case, these lists indicate what groups of authorities believe to be the books with the highest qualities and greatest interest for teenage readers. Among the awards are:

- Newbery Medal—the year's best book for children, selected by a committee of the American Library Association, usually with one or more "Honor Books," that is, runner-ups. (Sometimes the top choice is more appropriate for younger children—e.g., *Shiloh*; sometimes it's ideal for teenagers—e.g., *Jacob Have I Loved*; and sometimes it's appropriate for all levels—e.g., *The Giver*). The award is announced at the end of the ALA Midwinter Conference, held usually in late January or early February, and is noted immediately in major newspapers and later in most journals.

- Best Books for Young Adults—an extensive list of fiction and nonfiction, chosen by a committee of the American Library Association and published in the March issue of *School Library Journal*. (The Best of the Best from 1967 through 1992 were chosen during the summer of 1994.)
- Recommended Books for the Reluctant Young Adult Reader—selected annually by a committee of the American Library Association.
- *Boston Globe–Horn Book* Award—best books and honor books, fiction and nonfiction, announced in *Horn Book Magazine*.
- *School Library Journal* Best Books of the Year—published each December in *School Library Journal*.
- *Booklist* Editor's Choices—published each January in *Booklist*.
- *Horn Book* Fanfare Books—published each December in *Horn Book Magazine*.
- *Books for the Teenage*—selected each year by young adult librarians in the New York City Public Library System and published each March in a special booklet available from the New York Public Library.
- Golden Kite Award—a fiction and a nonfiction book chosen yearly by the Society of Children's Book Writers and Illustrators, often for younger readers but sometimes for teenagers (e.g., *Make Lemonade* in 1993).
- The IRA Children's Book Award—established in 1987 by the International Reading Association to recognize an outstanding book for older children.
- Coretta Scott King Award—winners and honor books feature African or African-American writers and characters.
- Young Adult Choices—books chosen by teenage readers through a regional selection process sponsored by the International Reading Association, published in the November issue of the *Journal of Reading*.
- Scott O'Dell Award for HistoricalFiction— administered by the *Bulletin for the Center for Children's Books*.
- Edgar Allan Poe Award, Young Adult Category—the year's best mystery, crime, or suspense novel from the Mystery Writers of America.

Look also for book awards in individual states, sponsored by library groups or associations of English and reading teachers. Among these are the California Young Reader's Medal, the Oregon Book Award for Young Readers, the Colorado Blue Spruce Young Adult Book Award, and the Texas Lone Star Reading List.

AUTHOR BIOGRAPHIES

For teachers and students who are seeking more information about favorite authors than dust-jacket blurbs provide, there are several sources. The most extensive information can be found in *Something about the Author* (*SATA*) and *Something about the Author Autobiography Series*, along with *Contemporary Authors*, all published by Gale Research Company. However, those sources are very expensive and not all school or public libraries can afford to keep up with each new volume in the series. Schools with up-to-date computer equipment should look into obtaining *SATA* on computer disks from Gale.

St. James Press in 1994 published an affordable one-volume edition of *Twentieth-Century Young Adult Writers* that contains biographical, bibliographical, and critical information on more than 400 authors of fiction, drama, and poetry for teenagers. Charles Scribner's Sons expects to publish a three-volume set of *Writers for Young Adults* in 1996, featuring critical biographies of 125 authors of books for young adults.

Even more affordable are two collections of autobiographies of authors of fiction for young adults, published by the National Council of Teachers of English: *Speaking for Ourselves: Autobiographical Sketches by Notable Authors of Books for Young Adults* (1990) and *Speaking for Ourselves, Too: More Autobiographical Sketches by Notable Authors of Books for Young Adults* (1993). These feature personal information about a combined total of 176 top authors in the field, with bibliographies and a photo of each author.

More extensive critical information about selected authors and their writings can be found in the Twayne Young Adult Author Series, each title beginning with *Presenting . . .* (as in *Presenting Walter Dean Myers* and *Presenting William Sleator*). Several of the books in this series have been updated and reissued in inexpensive paperback editions by Dell Publishing Company, including titles on Robert Cormier, S. E. Hinton, Norma Fox Mazer, M. E. Kerr, Rosa Guy, Judy Blume, and Richard Peck.

CONFERENCES AND WORKSHOPS

One of the most pleasurable aspects of developing an interest in books for young adults—as opposed to, say, becoming an expert on Chaucer, or the Brontë sisters, or William Faulkner—is that the authors in this field are *alive*. Not only can you read their works but you can also write to them, hear them speak at conferences, and talk with them personally as they autograph books for you in the exhibit hall of the convention center.

Part of the program of every national conference of the National Council of Teachers of English, the International Reading Association, and the American Library Association includes appearances by authors of books for children and young adults. The same is often true of regional and state conferences, although with smaller numbers. In addition to author appearances, other conference sessions are likely to focus on specific aspects of books for teenagers (e.g., new multicultural books for middle-school classrooms), and booksellers exhibit the latest titles of interest to young people.

The most extensive experience you can get in this field is by attending the two-day ALAN workshop that is part of the annual convention of the National Council of Teachers of English, held the week prior to Thanksgiving. For two solid days you can listen to individual authors and panels of experts talk about writing books for teenagers and teaching literature in grades 6 through 12. Each participant also receives a large package of books, usually one paperback from each of the dozen or so authors on the program. At the end of the first day there is a relaxing wine and cheese party at which you can chat with the authors as well as with other workshop participants. You might have the chance to meet such luminaries as Robert Cormier, Virginia Hamilton, Gary Paulsen, Sue Ellen Bridgers, M. E. Kerr, Bruce Brooks, or Walter Dean Myers, as well as some newer writers in the field. You will come away loaded with books, filled with new ideas, and invigorated by the possibilities.

You don't have to be a member of the sponsoring professional organizations in order to attend those conferences and workshops. But registration fees are usually lower for members, and it is through the journals, newsletters, and organizational mailings that those conferences are announced, so it pays to be a member.

COLLEAGUES

Although resources listed in textbooks are usually limited to published materials, we believe that one of the most valuable resources of all is the colleagues with whom we share common interests. If such people are in your building, so much the better. But they may even be on the other side of the country. The important thing is that you communicate with each other: through letters, through phone calls, or through the Internet. What have you read lately? What books are you teaching with the greatest success this year? What books seem to be most popular in your school right now?

Almost every time we, the authors of this book, talk with each other, one of us is likely to say "Have you read such-and-such yet?" or "What did you think of such-and-such?" When we talk with friends and colleagues across the country, we almost always mention our response to books they had recommended earlier and then suggest good books we've read recently. Sometimes we even swap copies of new books when we can't locate them in local stores for ourselves and can't wait another day to read the latest from Chris Crutcher, Paul Zindel, Ouida Sebestyen, or some hot new writer a publisher has just introduced to one of us.

If you don't yet have any friends who have discovered the joys of Young Adult Literature, be sure to attend one of the conferences we spoke about above; talk to people there, and find a new friend willing to correspond with you once or twice a year. Or register for a course on Young Adult Literature at your local college or university (assuming that such a course focuses on contemporary books and not on *Ivanhoe*, *Little Women*, and

Great Expectations), and team up with someone from that class who is willing to continue the dialogues you started there.

And as more schools come on-line with computers, you and your students can begin to communicate with other teachers and students in schools across the country, discussing books you have read and asking for their responses and recommendations. Your future sources for information can be worldwide and instantly available.

WORKS CITED

Titles that deal with multicultural themes or issues are preceded by an asterisk
(*). When possible, we have listed the softcover publisher. No publisher or
copyright date has been listed for works in the public domain.

PRIMARY SOURCES: MAJOR LITERARY WORKS

Adams, Douglas. *Hitchhiker's Guide to the Galaxy*. Pocket Books, 1991.
Allen, Thomas B. *Offerings at the Wall: Artifacts from the Veterans Memorial
        Collection*. Turner Publishing, 1995.
Appleman-Jurman, Alicia. *Alicia: My Story*. Bantam, 1988.
* Armstrong, William. *Sounder*. HarperCollins, 1989.
Arrick, Fran. *Tunnel Vision*. Dell, 1988.
_____ . *What You Don't Know Can Kill You*. Dell, 1994.
Ashabranner, Brent. *Always to Remember*. Scholastic, 1992.
Asher, Sandy. *Summer Smith Begins*. Bantam, 1987.
Avi. *Nothing But the Truth*. Avon, 1993.
* _____ . *The True Confessions of Charlotte Doyle*. Avon, 1992.
* Barrett, William. *Lilies of the Field*. Warner, 1988.
Beckett, Samuel. *Krapp's Last Tape*. Grove Press, 1970.
_____ . *Waiting for Godot*. Grove Press, 1954.
* Bell, William. *Forbidden City*. Bantam, 1991.
Betancourt, Jeanne. *More Than Meets the Eye*. Bantam, 1990.
* Block, Francesca Lia. *Weetzie Bat*. HarperCollins, 1989.
Blume, Judy. *Tiger Eyes*. Dell, 1982.
Bolt, Robert. *A Man For All Seasons*. Random House, 1962.
Bradbury, Ray. *Fahrenheit 451*. Ballantine, 1953.

Bridgers, Sue Ellen. *Home before Dark*. Bantam, 1985.

———. *Notes for Another Life*. Bantam, 1982.

———. *Permanent Connections*. Harper, 1987.

Brooks, Bruce. *Midnight Hour Encores*. Harper, 1988.

*———. *The Moves Make the Man*. Harper, 1987.

———. *What Hearts*. HarperCollins, 1992.

Brooks, Martha. *Two Moons in August*. Scholastic, 1993.

Bunting, Eve. *The Wall*. Clarion, 1990.

* Buss, Fran Leeper. *Journey of the Sparrows*. Dell, 1993.

Camus, Albert. *The Stranger*. Knopf, 1946.

* Cannon, A. E. *Amazing Gracie*. Dell, 1993.

Carter, Alden R. *Dancing on Dark Waters*. Scholastic, 1990.

———. *Sheila's Dying*. Scholastic, 1989.

———. *Up Country*. Scholastic, 1991.

* Cary, Lorene. *Black Ice*. Vintage, 1992.

* Childress, Alice. *Rainbow Jordan*. Avon, 1982.

Chute, Nevil. *On the Beach*. Ballantine, 1983.

Clapp, Patricia. *Witches' Children: A Story of Salem*. Lothrop, Lee, and Shepard, 1982.

Cole, Brock. *Celine*. Farrar, Straus & Giroux, 1989.

*———. *The Goats*. Farrar, Straus & Giroux, 1987.

Collier, James Lincoln. *When the Stars Begin to Fall*. Dell, 1989.

Coman, Carolyn. *Tell Me Everything*. Farrar, Straus & Giroux, 1992.

Cooney, Caroline B. *Driver's Ed*. Delacorte, 1994.

———. *Flight #116 Is Down*. Scholastic, 1992.

Cormier, Robert. *The Bumblebee Flies Anyway*. Dell, 1991.

———. *The Chocolate War*. Dell, 1986.

———. *I Am the Cheese*. Dell, 1991.

———. *Tunes for Bears to Dance To*. Dell, 1994.

———. *We All Fall Down*. Dell, 1993.

Cottonwood, Joe. *Quake!* Scholastic, 1995.

* Covington, Dennis. *Lizard*. Dell, 1993.

Crane, Stephen. *The Red Badge of Courage*.

* Crew, Linda. *Children of the River*. Dell, 1991.

Crutcher, Chris. *Chinese Handcuffs*. Dell, 1991.

*———. *The Crazy Horse Electric Game*. Dell, 1988.

———. *Ironman*. Greenwillow, 1995.

*———. *Running Loose*. Dell, 1986.

———. *Staying Fat for Sarah Byrnes*. Dell, 1995.

*———. *Stotan!* Dell, 1986.

Cushman, Karen. *Catherine, Called Birdy*. HarperCollins, 1995.

———. *The Midwife's Apprentice*. Clarion, 1995.

Daly, Maureen. *Seventeenth Summer*. Dodd, Mead, 1942.

Davis, Jenny. *Checking on the Moon*. Dell, 1993.

———. *Sex Education*. Dell, 1989.

Davis, Terry. *If Rock and Roll Were a Machine*. Dell, 1994.

———. *Vision Quest*. Dell, 1994.

* Denenberg, Barry. *Voices from Vietnam*. Scholastic, 1994.

Deuker, Carl. *On the Devil's Court*. Avon, 1991.

Dickens, Charles. *Great Expectations*.

———. *A Tale of Two Cities*.

Dickinson, Peter. *Eva*. Dell, 1991.

Dillard, Annie. *Pilgrim at Tinker Creek*. Bantam, 1975.

Doherty, Berlie. *Dear Nobody*. Orchard, 1992.

Duder, Tessa. *In Lane Three Alex Archer*. Bantam, 1991.

Duncan, Lois. *Killing Mr. Griffin*. Dell, 1990.

Edelman, Bernard, ed. *Dear America: Letters Home from Vietnam*. Pocket Books, 1989.

Ehrlich, Amy. *Where It Stops, Nobody Knows*. Puffin, 1990.

Eliot, George. *Silas Marner*.

* Ellison, Ralph. *The Invisible Man*. Random House, 1952.

Fast, Howard. *April Morning*. Morrow, 1972.

———. *The Hessian*. Morrow, 1972.

Felsen, Henry Gregor. *Crash Club*. Random House, 1958.

———. *Hot Rod*. Dutton, 1950.

———. *Street Rod*. Random House, 1953.

———. *Two and the Town*. Scribner's, 1952.

Fitzgerald, F. Scott. *The Great Gatsby*.

Fleischman, Paul. *The Borning Room*. HarperCollins, 1993.

* ———. *Saturnalia*. HarperCollins, 1992.

* Foote, Shelby. *Shiloh*. Vintage, 1991.

Forbes, Esther. *Johnny Tremain*. Houghton Mifflin, 1943.

* Fox, Paula. *Monkey Island*. Dell, 1993.

———. *One-Eyed Cat*. Dell, 1993.

* ———. *The Slave Dancer*. Dell, 1991.

Frank, Anne. *The Diary of a Young Girl*. Pocket Books, 1990.

* Gaines, Ernest J. *The Autobiography of Miss Jane Pittman*. Bantam, 1982.

* Gallo, Donald R., ed. *Sixteen: Short Stories by Outstanding Writers for Young Adults*. Dell, 1985.

* ———. *Ultimate Sports: Short Stories by Outstanding Writers for Young Adults*. Delacorte, 1995.

Gardner, John. *Grendel*. Knopf, 1971.

* George, Jean Craighead. *Julie of the Wolves*. Harper, 1974.

* Gibbons, Kaye. *Ellen Foster*. Vintage, 1990.

Gies, Miep, and Alison Leslie Gold. *Anne Frank Remembered*. Simon and Schuster, 1987.

Go Ask Alice. Avon, 1972.

Golding, William. *Lord of the Flies*. Putnam, 1954.

* Goldman, Peter, and Tony Fuller. *Charlie Company: What Vietnam Did to Us*. Morrow, 1983.

Greene, Bette. *The Drowning of Stephan Jones*. Bantam, 1992.

———. *Summer of My German Soldier*. Dell, 1993.

Guest, Judith. *Ordinary People*. Penguin, 1982.

* Guy, Rosa. *The Friends*. Bantam, 1994.

* Hamilton, Virginia. *Many Thousand Gone: African Americans from Slavery to Freedom*. Knopf, 1993.

*———. *Plain City*. Scholastic, 1994.

*———. *Sweet Whispers, Brother Rush*. Avon, 1993.

*Hansen, Joyce. *Out from This Place*. Avon, 1992.

———. *Which Way Freedom?* Avon, 1992.

Hawthorne, Nathaniel. *The Scarlet Letter*.

Heller, Joseph. *Catch 22*. Dell, 1990.

Hemingway, Ernest. *The Old Man and the Sea*. Scribner's, 1952.

*Hentoff, Nat. *The Day They Came to Arrest the Book*. Delacorte, 1982.

*———. *Jazz Country*. Harper, 1965.

Hesse, Karen. *Phoenix Rising*. Holt, 1994.

Hinton, S. E. *The Outsiders*. Dell, 1989.

———. *Rumblefish*. Dell, 1989.

———. *That Was Then, This Is Now*. Dell, 1989.

*Hobbs, Will. *Beardance*. Atheneum, 1993.

*———. *Changes in Latitude*. Avon, 1993.

*———. *Downriver*. Atheneum, 1991.

Hoffius, Stephen. *Winners and Losers*. Simon and Schuster, 1993.

Holman, Felice. *Slake's Limbo*. Dell, 1977.

Homer. *The Odyssey*.

Homes, A. M. *Jack*. Vintage, 1990.

*Houston, Jean Wakatsuki, and James D. Houston. *Farewell to Manzanar*. Bantam, 1990.

Hunt, Irene. *No Promises in the Wind*. Berkeley, 1986.

*Hudson, Jan. *Sweetgrass*. Scholastic, 1991.

*Hurston, Zora Neale. *Their Eyes Were Watching God*. University of Illinois Press, 1978.

Jenson, Kathryn. *Pocket Change*. Scholastic, 1991.

*Johnson, Angela. *Toning the Sweep*. Scholastic, 1994.

Kerr, M. E. *Deliver Us from Evie*. HarperCollins, 1995.

———. *Dinky Hocker Shoots Smack!* Harper & Row, 1972.

———. *Gentlehands*. Harper, 1990.

———. *Night Kites*. Harper, 1987.

Klass, David. *California Blue*. Scholastic, 1994.

———. *Wrestling with Honor*. Scholastic, 1991.

Klause, Annette Curtis. *The Silver Kiss*. Dell, 1992.

Klein, Norma. *Mom, the Wolfman and Me*. Pantheon, 1972.

Knowles, John. *A Separate Peace*. Bantam, 1982.

*Krisher, Trudy. *Spite Fences*. Delacorte, 1994.

*Lasky, Kathryn. *Beyond the Divide*. Dell, 1986.

———. *Memoirs of a Bookbat*. Harcourt Brace, 1994.

*Lee, Harper. *To Kill a Mockingbird*. Warner, 1960.

Levenkron, Steven. *The Best Little Girl in the World*. Warner, 1989.

*Levine, Ellen. *Freedom's Children: Young Civil Rights Activists Tell Their Own Stories*. Avon, 1994.

Levy, Marilyn. *Rumors and Whispers*. Fawcett, 1990.

*Lipsyte, Robert. *The Brave*. Harper, 1993.

———. *The Chemo Kid*. HarperCollins, 1993.

*———. *The Chief*. Harper, 1993.

*_____ . *The Contender*. HarperCollins, 1987.

London, Jack. *The Call of the Wild*. Macmillan, 1963.

Lowry, Lois. *The Giver*. Dell, 1994.

_____ . *Number the Stars*. Dell, 1990.

Lund, Doris. *Eric*. Dell, 1990.

Lynch, Chris. *Iceman*. HarperCollins, 1994.

_____ . *Shadowboxer*. HarperCollins, 1994.

Mahy, Margaret. *The Changeover*. Puffin, 1994.

_____ . *Memory*. Dell, 1989.

Malmgren, Dallin. *The Ninth Issue*. Delacorte, 1989.

_____ . *The Whole Nine Yards*. Dell, 1987.

Marsden, John. *So Much to Tell You*. Joy Street Books, 1989.

Mason, Bobbie Ann. *In Country*. Harper Perennial, 1986.

Matas, Carol. *Daniel's Story*. Scholastic, 1993.

Mazer, Harry. *The Last Mission*. Dell, 1990.

Mazer, Norma Fox. *Out of Control*. Avon, 1994.

_____ . *Silver*. Avon, 1989.

Mazer, Norma Fox, and Harry Mazer. *Bright Days, Stupid Nights*. Dell, 1993.

McKinley, Robin. *The Hero and the Crown*. Berkeley, 1986.

*McKissick, Patricia C., and Frederick McKissick. *Sojourner Truth: Ain't I a Woman?* Scholastic, 1992.

Miklowitz, Gloria D. *After the Bomb*. Scholastic, 1987.

_____ . Anything to Win. Dell, 1990.

Miller, Arthur. *The Crucible*. Dramatists Play Service, 1982.

_____ . *Death of a Salesman*. Dramatists Play Service, 1980.

* Morrison, Toni. *The Bluest Eye*. Pocket Books, 1972.

Murphy, Jim. *The Long Road to Gettysburg*. Clarion, 1992.

* Murrow, Liza Ketchum. *Twelve Days in August*. Holiday House, 1993.

* Myers, Walter Dean. *Fallen Angels*. Scholastic, 1989.

*_____ . *Hoops*. Dell, 1990.

*_____ . *Scorpions*. Harper, 1988.

*_____ . *Somewhere in the Darkness*. Scholastic, 1992.

Naughton, Jim. *My Brother Stealing Second*. Harper, 1991.

O'Brien, Robert C. *Z for Zachariah*. Macmillan, 1987.

* O'Brien, Tim. *The Things They Carried*. Penguin, 1991.

O'Dell, Scott. *Sarah Bishop*. Scholastic, 1982.

Oneal, Zibby. *In Summer Light*. Viking, 1985.

_____ . *The Language of Goldfish*. Puffin, 1990.

O'Neill, Eugene. *Ah, Wilderness!* Harper, 1939.

_____ . *Mourning Becomes Electra*. Vintage, 1959.

Orwell, George. *Nineteen Eighty-Four*. Monarch Press, 1985.

Palmer, Laura. *Shrapnel in the Heart: Letters and Remembrances from the Vietnam Memorial*. Random House, 1988.

* Parks, Rosa. *Rosa Parks: My Story*. Dial, 1992.

Paterson, Katherine. *Jacob Have I Loved*. Crowell, 1980.

_____ . *Lyddie*. Puffin, 1992.

_____ . *Park's Quest*. Puffin, 1989.

* Paulsen, Gary. *The Crossing*. Dell, 1990.

*_____. *Dogsong*. Bradbury, 1985.

_____. *Harris and Me*. Harcourt Brace, 1993.

_____. *Hatchet*. Puffin, 1988.

_____. *The Island*. Dell, 1990.

_____. *The Monument*. Dell, 1993.

*_____. *Mr. Tucket*. Delacorte, 1994.

*_____. *Nightjohn*. Dell, 1995.

_____. *The River*. Dell, 1993.

_____. *The Voyage of the Frog*. Dell, 1990.

_____. *Woodsong*. Puffin, 1991.

Peck, Richard. *Princess Ashley*. Dell, 1988.

_____. *Remembering the Good Times*. Dell, 1986.

_____. *Unfinished Portrait of Jessica*. Dell, 1993.

*Peck, Robert Newton. *Arly*. Scholastic, 1991.

*_____. *Arly's Run*. Walker and Co., 1991.

_____. *A Day No Pigs Would Die*. Dell, 1979.

_____. *A Part of the Sky*. Knopf, 1994.

*Petry, Ann. *Tituba of Salem Village*. HarperCollins, 1991.

Pfeffer, Susan Beth. *The Year without Michael*. Bantam, 1987.

Pierce, Tamara. *Alanna*. Knopf, 1989.

_____. *In the Hands of the Goddess*. Knopf, 1990.

_____. *Lioness Rampant*. Knopf, 1990.

_____. *The Woman Who Rides Like a Man*. Knopf, 1990.

Potok, Chaim. *The Chosen*. Fawcett, 1978.

Pullman, Philip. *Ruby in the Smoke*. Knopf, 1988.

_____. *Shadow in the North*. Knopf, 1988.

_____. *The Tiger in the Well*. Knopf, 1992.

Remarque, Erich Maria. *All Quiet on the Western Front*.

Renault, Mary. *The King Must Die*. Pantheon, 1958.

Rinaldi, Ann. *A Break with Charity: A Story about Salem*. Harcourt Brace, 1994.

*_____. *In My Father's House*. Scholastic, 1993.

_____. *The Last Silk Dress*. Bantam, 1990.

_____. *A Stitch in Time*. Scholastic, 1994.

*_____. *Wolf by the Ears*. Scholastic, 1993.

Rogasky, Barbara. *Smoke and Ashes: The Story of the Holocaust*. Holiday, 1988.

Rostand, Edmond. *Cyrano de Bergerac*. Modern Library, 1951.

Rylant, Cynthia. *Missing May*. Dell, 1992.

Salinger, J. D. *The Catcher in the Rye*. Bantam, 1964.

*Salisbury, Graham. *Under the Blood-Red Sun*. Delacorte, 1995.

*Sebestyen, Ouida. *Words by Heart*. Bantam, 1990.

Sendar, Ruth. *The Cage*. Macmillan, 1986.

Shakespeare, William. *Hamlet*.

_____. *Julius Caesar*.

_____. *Macbeth*.

_____. *Romeo and Juliet*.

*Shange, Ntozake. *Betsey Brown: A Novel*. St. Martin's, 1985.

Siegel, Aranka. *Upon the Head of a Goat*. Puffin, 1994.

*Sleator, William. *The Boy Who Reversed Himself*. Dutton, 1986.

_____ . *House of Stairs*. Puffin, 1991.

_____ . *Interstellar Pig*. Bantam, 1986.

_____ . *Others See Us*. Dutton, 1993.

_____ . *Strange Attractors*. Puffin, 1991.

Smiley, Jane. *A Thousand Acres*. Random House, 1991.

Sophocles. *Antigone*.

Speare, Elizabeth George. *The Witch of Blackbird Pond*. Dell, 1987.

Spiegelman, Art. *Maus: A Survivor's Tale*. Pantheon, 1986.

* Spinelli, Jerry. *Maniac Magee*. Harper, 1992.

_____ . *Night of the Whale*. Dell, 1988.

_____ . *There's a Girl in My Hammerlock*. Simon and Schuster, 1993.

* Staples, Suzanne Fisher. *Shabanu*. Knopf, 1991.

Steinbeck, John. *The Grapes of Wrath*.

_____ . *Of Mice and Men*.

Stevermer, Caroline. *River Rats*. Harcourt Brace Jovanovich, 1992.

Strasser, Todd. *Rock 'n' Roll Nights*. Dell, 1982.

_____ . *The Wave*. Dell, 1981.

Swarthout, Glendon. *Bless the Beasts and Children*. Doubleday, 1970.

Sweeney, Joyce. *Shadow*. Delacorte, 1994.

Talbert, Marc. *The Purple Heart*. Harper, 1992.

Tamar, Erika.*The Things I Did Last Summer*. Harcourt Brace, 1994.

Tan, Amy. *The Joy Luck Club*. Thorndike Press, 1989.

* Taylor, Mildred D. *Let the Circle Be Unbroken*. Puffin, 1991.

*_____ . *The Road to Memphis*. Puffin, 1992.

*_____ . *Roll of Thunder, Hear My Cry*. Puffin, 1991.

* Terry, Wallace. *Bloods: An Oral History of the Vietnam War by Black Veterans*.
          Ballantine, 1992.

Thesman, Jean. *Where the Road Ends*. Avon, 1993.

Thoreau, Henry David. *Walden*.

Tolkien, J.R.R. *The Fellowship of the Ring*. Houghton Mifflin, 1965.

_____ . *Lord of the Rings*. Houghton Mifflin, 1965.

Tunis, John. *Iron Duke*. Harcourt Brace, 1938.

* Twain, Mark. *The Adventures of Huckleberry Finn*.

_____ . *Tom Sawyer*.

Tyler, Anne. *Dinner at the Homesick Restaurant*. Random House, 1982.

Uchida, Yoshiko. *The Invisible Thread*. Simon and Schuster, 1991.

Vining, Elizabeth Gray. *Adam of the Road*. Puffin, 1987.

* Voigt, Cynthia. *Dicey's Song*. Fawcett, 1987.

*_____ . *Homecoming*. Fawcett, 1987.

*_____ . *The Runner*. Fawcett, 1987.

_____ . *Tell Me If the Lovers Are Losers*. Fawcett, 1987.

_____ . *When She Hollers*. Scholastic, 1994.

Vonnegut, Kurt, Jr. *Slaughterhouse Five*. Laurel, 1968.

* Walker, Alice. *The Color Purple*. Pocket Books, 1988.

* Walter, Mildred Pitts. *The Girl on the Outside*. Scholastic, 1993.

* Watkins, Yoko Kawashima. *So Far from the Bamboo Grove*. Puffin, 1987.

Wells, Rosemary. *When No One Was Looking*. Scholastic, 1991.

Wharton, Edith. *Ethan Frome*. Scribner's, 1970.

White, Ellen Emerson. *The Road Home*. Scholastic, 1995.

Wilder, Thornton. *Our Town*. Harper, 1960.

Williams, Tennessee. *The Glass Menagerie*. Dramatists Play Service, 1975.

* Williams-Garcia, Rita. *Blue Tights*. Bantam, 1989.

* Wolff, Virginia Euwer. *Make Lemonade*. Scholastic, 1994.

———. *The Mozart Season*. Scholastic, 1993.

* Yep, Laurence. *Dragon's Gate*. HarperCollins, 1993.

Yolen, Jane. *Briar Rose*. T. Doherty Assoc., 1992.

Zindel, Paul. *Harry and Hortense at Hormone High*. Bantam, 1985.

———. *The Pigman*. Bantam, 1983.

SECONDARY SOURCES: BOOKS AND MONOGRAPHS

Adamson, Lynda G. *Recreating the Past: A Guide to American and World Historical Fiction for Children and Young Adults*. Westport, CT: Greenwood Press, 1994.

Applebee, Arthur N. *A Study of Book-Length Works Taught in High School English Courses*. Albany: State University of New York, 1989.

Bushman, Kay Parks. *A Thematic Guide to Young Adult Literature—Annotations, Critiques and Sources*. Ottawa, KS: The Writing Conference Inc., 1993.

Carlsen, G. Robert. *Books and the Teenage Reader*, 2nd rev. ed. New York: Bantam Books, 1980.

Carlsen, G. Robert, and Anne Sherrill. *Voices of Readers: How We Come to Love Books*. Urbana, IL: National Council of Teachers of English, 1988.

Carter, Betty. *Best Books for Young Adults*. Chicago: American Library Association, 1994.

Donelson, Kenneth, and Alleen Pace Nilsen. *Literature for Today's Young Adults*, 3rd ed. Glenview, IL: Scott, Foresman, 1989.

Estes, Sally. *Genre Favorites for Young Adults*. Chicago: American Library Association, 1993.

———. *Growing Up Is Hard to Do*. Chicago: American Library Association, 1994.

Gallo, Donald R., ed. *Literature for Teenagers: New Books, New Approaches* (*Connecticut English Journal*, Fall 1993). Urbana, IL: NCTE, 1993.

Gillespie, John T. *Best Books for Junior High Readers*. New York: R. R. Bowker, 1991.

Helbig, Althea K., and Agnes Regan Perkins. *This Land Is Our Land: A Guide to Multicultural Literature for Children and Young Adults*. Westport, CT: Greenwood Press, 1994.

Jung, C. G. *The Archetypes and the Collective Unconscious*. Princeton, NJ: Princeton University Press, 1969.

Kaywell, Joan F., ed. *Adolescent Literature as a Complement to the Classics*. Norwood, MA: Christopher Gordon Publishers, Vol. 1, 1993; Vol. 2, 1994.

———. *Adolescents at Risk: A Guide to Fiction and Nonfiction for Young Adults, Parents, and Professionals*. Westport, CT: Greenwood Press, 1993.

McBride, William G., ed. *High Interest, Easy Reading: A Booklist for Junior and Senior High School Students*, 6th ed. Urbana, IL: NCTE, 1990.

Moir, Hughes, ed. *Collected Perspectives: Choosing and Using Books for the Classroom*, 2nd ed. Norwood, MA: Christopher Gordon Publishers, 1992.

Probst, Robert E. *Response and Analysis: Teaching Literature in Junior and Senior High School*. Portsmouth, NH: Boynton/Cook, 1988.

Rochman, Hazel. *Against Borders: Promoting Books for a Multicultural World*. Chicago: American Library Association, 1993.

Rosenblatt, Louise M. *Literature as Exploration*, 4th ed. New York: Modern Language Association, 1983.

———. *The Reader, the Text, the Poem*. Carbondale: Southern Illinois University Press, 1978.

Spencer, Pam. *What Do Young Adults Read Next? A Reader's Guide to Fiction for Young Adults*. Detroit: Gale Research Inc., 1994.

Webb, C. Anne, ed. *Your Reading: A Booklist for Junior High and Middle School*, 9th ed. Urbana, IL: NCTE, 1993.

Williams, Helen E. *Books by African-American Authors and Illustrators for Children and Young Adults*. Chicago: American Library Association, 1991.

Wurth, Shirley, ed. *Books for You: A Booklist for Senior High Students*, 11th ed. Urbana, IL: NCTE, 1992.

Zvirin, Stephanie. *The Best Years of Their Lives: A Resource Guide for Teenagers in Crisis*. Chicago: American Library Association, 1992.

SECONDARY SOURCES: ARTICLES, POEMS, AND CHAPTERS FROM BOOKS

Brown, Margaret, and Pat Muller. "TAB: A Middle School/Public Library Success Story." *VOYA (Voice of Youth Advocates)*, December 1994: 255–258.

Carlsen, G. Robert. "Literature Is." *English Journal* 63 (1974): 23–27.

Finney, Kay (in collaboration with Kim McCombs). "Teenagers Work Well in the Berkeley Public Library." *VOYA*, April 1994: 11–14.

Gallo, Donald R. "Listening to Readers: Attitudes toward the Young Adult Novel." In *Reading Their World*, eds. Virginia R. Monseau and Gary M. Salvner (Portsmouth, NH: Boynton/Cook, 1992), 17–27.

George, Phil. "Battle Won Is Lost." In *Zero Makes Me Hungry: A Collection of Poems for Today*, eds. Edward Leuders and Primus St. John (Glenview, IL: Scott, Foresman, and Co., 1976), 106.

Mazer, Harry. "Furlough 1944." *In Sixteen: Short Stories by Outstanding Writers for Young Adults*, ed. Donald R. Gallo (Dell, 1985), 83–91.

Owen, Wilfred. "Dolce Et Decorum Est."

Sandburg, Carl. "Grass." In *Harvest Poems* (New York: Harcourt, Brace and World, 1960), 51–52.

Small, Robert C. "The Literary Value of the Young Adult Novel." *Journal of Youth Services in Libraries*, Spring 1992: 227–285.

Sprince, Leila J. "For Young Adults Only: Tried and True Youth Participation Manual." *VOYA*, October 1994: 197–199.

INDEX

About the Authors

SARAH K. HERZ has taught English in the seventh through twelfth grades in the Westport, Connecticut school system for twenty-three years. She is on the board of directors of the Connecticut Council of Teachers of English. She frequently conducts teacher workshops on young adult literature and has published articles on young adult literature in *Classroom Practices in Teaching English* (a publication of the National Council of Teachers of English) and *Connecticut English Journal*. Herz has been a recipient of fellowships from the National Endowment for the Humanities and the Connecticut Humanities Council.

DONALD R. GALLO is Professor of English at Central Connecticut State University and is editor of seven collections of short stories written by well-known authors of young adult literature. The most recent of these is *Ultimate Sports*. The first, *Sixteen*, was named by the American Library Association as one of the one hundred Best of the Best Books for Young Adults published between 1967 and 1992. He is also editor/compiler of two volumes of autobiographies of authors of young adult literature, *Speaking for Ourselves* (1990) and *Speaking for Ourselves, Too* (1993), and of *Literature for Teenagers: New Books, New Approaches* (1993). Among his other works are *Authors' Insights: Turning Teenagers into Readers and Writers* (1992), *Center Stage: One-Act Plays for Teenage Readers and Actors* (1990), and *Presenting Richard Peck* (1989).